For Joe
my young cousin—
Here are some
unexplored insights
for finding something
big to live for.

George

D0181177

Where Did We Come From and Where Are We Going?

Books by GEORGE BOCKL

SECULAR:

George Bockl on Investment Real Estate
How Real Estate Fortunes Are Made
How to Use Leverage to Make Money in Local Real Estate
Recycling Real Estate:
The Number-One Way to Make Money in the '80s

SPIRITUAL:

God beyond Religion
How to Find Something Big to Live For
Living beyond Success
Universal Spirituality
Where Did We Come From and Where Are We Going?

Where Did We Come From and Where Are We Going?

In Search of a Road to Universal Spirituality

GEORGE BOCKL

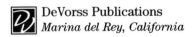 DeVorss Publications
Marina del Rey, California

Where Did We Come From and Where Are We Going?

© 2000 George Bockl

All rights reserved. No part of this book may be reproduced or transmitted in any form without permission in writing from the publisher, except by a reviewer who may quote brief passages for review purposes.

ISBN: 087516-732-2
Library of Congress Catalog Card Number 99-76973
First Edition, 2000

DeVorss & Company
Box 550
Marina del Rey CA 90294

Printed in the United States of America

DEDICATED TO

The Pioneers of the Coming
Universal Spiritual Revolution

INTRODUCTION

The Prophets have made giant tracks on the pathless unknown, and millions have followed in their footsteps. While their prophetic conjectures have penetrated close to God's reality, their claims have not been proven. That's because the unfathomable is not subject to proof.

Since civilization began, man has been trying to wrest meaning out of the invisible. The early Greeks, the mystics, and the founders of various religions have left their indelible marks on civilization, but the tracks of the noisy false prophets have been blown over by the sands of history and forgotten.

I'm not a scholar or a theologian. I'm a successful real-estate developer with a curiosity to find a new challenge beyond success. I found it in speculations on spirituality and the pathless unknown. Over the years, therefore, I have filled thirty-seven 100-page notebooks with meditative notes on the spiritual conjectures of people from many cultures, as well as my own, about what ought to be my relationship to God, man, and the universe.

Some of the ruminations from the East were intriguingly new to me. Eastern wisdom departs from mainstream Western religion by claiming that life is a constant becoming, reincarnation after reincarnation, with a never-ending evolutionary journey as our destiny.

My biblical beliefs about the coming of the Messiah have been replaced by new views: that the universe is a living entity powered by cosmic energy; that it sustains its parts with an underlying law of periodicity, where cycles of birth and death are governed by an ever-progressing law of evolution; that the concept of an anthropomorphic God is transmuted into the belief that God is the body of the universe, and its Cosmic Wisdom creates, pervades, and guides all its entities.

My aim is to examine many subjects in succinct form, emphasizing their core essence rather than embellishing a few with elaborate detail. I will present ideas to you, the reader, that I hope may challenge, intrigue, and perhaps even shock you—ideas that will stimulate new thinking and move forward, in a constructive way, your effort to understand and reach for the unknown.

George Bockl

My use of the words man and mankind is for the sake of simplicity only, and does not in any way represent a slight toward women.

CONTENTS

Part 1

PART

1

Universal Spirituality

Chapter 1

My Odyssey in Search of

Purposeful Living

It began during the aftermath of the Russian Revolution when, as a child, I was forced to feel the fright of my elders from pogroms, marauding bandits, and officials who sent to Siberia anyone suspected of anticommunism.

My mother and I escaped Russia in 1920 by crossing the border into Poland in a smuggler's haywagon. We cowered in fear because communist patrols killed escaping refugees on sight. After wandering across Europe for two years, we finally obtained a visa. We crossed the Atlantic, sardined in filth in the bowels of a ship, and arrived in America seventeen days later. So at age twelve, illiterate and in a foreign land, I began my education. Later, there were three agonizing years when I couldn't find employment. At last I got a foothold in selling and developing real estate.

By 1950, I had become wealthy beyond my wildest expectations. But then something traumatic occurred in the form of two radical transformations in my mind: my orthodox religion lost its salt, and, more drastic, an ennui set in that sapped my desire to add new layers of success to my life. It was like wandering in a fog. Having left traditional religion, and without enthusiasm for business, I felt as if in a vacuum of purposeless living.

Moral Rearmament

In this frame of mind, I found myself on vacation with my family on Mackinac Island, Michigan. I took a walk and saw a "Moral Rearmament" sign on a building. The embryo of my spiritual awakening was formed right there when I discovered a world Moral Rearmament (MRA)

conference in full session. About a thousand people—
from many countries, religions, and races; business people, politicians, and labor leaders; white, black, and
brown—had come to find the common denominator of
universal morality based on the four standards of absolute
unselfishness, honesty, purity, and love.

At this conference and at a dozen others I attended
over several years, I met people with whom I discussed
in depth the meaning of morality. I learned how people
had experienced revolutionary changes in their natures
when they sought guidance from God during a daily
hour of quiet time. I had a one-on-one dialog with a
Zulu chief from South Africa, a teacher from Burma, an
electrician from England, and a student from Japan. I
talked with an archaeologist from New York, a one-time
Italian communist, a former SS trooper from Nazi
Germany, and Rajmahah Gandhi, grandson of India's
Mahatma Gandhi, as well as many others. Truly my
mind was caught up in a heady, glorious whirl. I had
met a new breed of human being.

Theosophy

Several years later, my mind was kindled by another spectacular idea. A tenant in one of my buildings introduced
me to the concept of Theosophy (wisdom of God). It
turned my previously held religious ideas topsy-turvy and
opened spiritual vistas beyond Moral Rearmament.
While MRA dealt with how to change our human nature,
Theosophy conjectured about the deeper aspects of life.
It toppled old beliefs and replaced them with startling
revolutionary ones.

I plunged into copious reading of theosophical literature by writers from many countries—there are Theosophy Chapters in some fifty nations. I attended lectures by leaders from various cultures, races, and religions and discussed their ideas with them. I was deeply impressed by the following undergirding cosmic principles in Theosophy:

What we generally refer to as God is ubiquitous Cosmic Energy that has intentionality, purpose, and intelligence.

The universe is the body of God, One Life, and all entities within it are its organs.

The prime purpose of God (Cosmic Energy) is constant creation, generating new forms and expanding the consciousness of its creatures.

Evolution is Cosmic Energy's vehicle for fueling and advancing its creativity.

Periodicity, cyclicity, and especially reincarnation light up man's future with the radiance of immortality.

Universal Spirituality—distinctly different from sectarian religious spirituality—is the new progressive evolutionary ideal for our time, just as the One God ideal, the Ten Commandments, and Jesus' "Love One Another" were the progressive evolutionary ideals for their times.

For me, these theosophical insights defined my new role in the universe; it was a momentous change. I bid an appreciative goodbye to the mythological religious wisdom that had stabilized the early years of my life and said an excited hello to the uncertainties awaiting me in my ongoing quest for a new vision of God.

Christian Science

I didn't stop with Theosophy. I wanted to learn all I could about other insightful concepts that would give me a more profound vision of life's meaning. My friend Gordon Smith knew nothing about Moral Rearmament or Theosophy, but he was on fire with a belief that shone brightly in one of the godliest men I have ever known. His ultimate ideal was Christian Science. Gordon inspired me to attend dozens of Sunday lectures and to read *Science and Health,* by Mary Baker Eddy. In my view, the main thrust of its wisdom was to clarify the difference between mortal mind and Divine Mind. The former is described as the "murky machinations" of man's illusory groping for reality, while Divine Mind is the only Reality, within which we live and have our being.

Christian Science literature is replete with persuasive proof of how Divine Mind heals the body, calms the emotions, and clarifies the mind. Gordon Smith was healed of cancer of the esophagus. I came to know many of his fellow believers and saw a convincing difference between those who flounder in mortal mind and the Christian Scientists, who attempt to conduct their lives according to what they understand of Divine Mind.

Other Groups

My renewed interest in real-estate development involved me with prominent people who happened to be Unitarians. Could it be that Unitarianism held the answer to uniting the fragmented religions? I wondered. After attending several dozen Sunday services, I came away with the feeling that the minister and the congregation were more interested in discussing social issues than in how to unite religions. God seemed to be on the back burner.

My secretary was a Jehovah's Witness who diplomatically hinted that I could be saved from perdition only if I believed in the Second Coming of Christ. To please her, I attended several Jehovah's Witness services. In contrast to the Unitarians, who were immaculately dressed, the congregation came in working clothes. Their camaraderie and effusive friendliness—after they listened attentively to a sermon about the heavenly bliss in the afterlife—burst into a joyous demonstration. Their absolute faith inspired them to live extraordinarily moral lives. Could my conjectural views about a cosmic-energy God, evolution, reincarnation, and Universal Spirituality motivate them the way that their religious certainties did? I wondered, but couldn't help doubting it.

I became interested in the Baha'i faith through a Jewish friend who told me that he went to Baha'i because it was an extension of Judaism. Baha-Ullah, my friend told me, is the prophet for our time as previous prophets were for their times.

Baha-Ullah's principal revelations are: the future oneness of religion, the equality of men and women, the harmony of science and religion, the elimination of extreme wealth and poverty, the protection of cultural diversity, and world government. The Baha'i faith has followers in 132 countries, and four million people are incorporating the teachings into their lives. I attended several of their meetings, but I was not comfortable with their belief in an anthropomorphic God and in a heavenly-abode afterlife.

What I learned from these breakaway religions is that there are many wise ways to find God-fulfillment and to elevate the quality of one's life. The problem mankind faces, however, is that while all religions inspire their members to care for one another within their boundaries, they have as yet not inspired them to care for those outside their boundaries. The tragic fact is that the virtues that religions generate within their borders become vices outside their borders.

What transcendent spirit could inspire the Jews and Arabs in the Middle East, the Catholics and Protestants in Northern Ireland, Muslims and Hindus in Pakistan and India to come out of their enclosures and seek solutions to their hostilities? The answer, in my humble view, is "Universal Spirituality," the next phase beyond particularized religious wisdom.

Chapter **2**

What Is Universal

Spirituality?

Universal Spirituality is different from traditional religions because it transcends creeds, cults, gurus, and codes of behavior. Religion has boundaries set by scriptures, traditions, holy places, and authoritarian institutions. There are rules that define a particular religion and in turn define the beliefs of its members.

Universal Spirituality is not like that. It could more easily be defined as an attitude that involves an unending quest for truth—whatever it may turn out to be on the journey of discovery. It does not offer definite answers to questions or an obligatory way to live in a community of shared beliefs. It is not a comfortable religious haven.

To arrive at Universal Spirituality, the spiritual explorer must take an uncharted path with no scriptural guidance except the insights gained from personal experiences.

Men and women who were disenchanted with dogmatic religions planted the seeds of Universal Spirituality about a century ago. Prominent among them were Mme. Blavatsky of Russia, Annie Besant of England, Col. Olcott of America, J. Krishnamurti of India, Emmet Fox and Ernest Holmes of America. All were revolutionary luminaries who dared to question centuries-old religious certainties.

The lectures, discussions, and writings of these inspired teachers are the seeds that have sprouted into shoots in many countries. Students form study groups, and when the numbers become too large, they form groups under such names as Theosophy, Religious Science, Science of Mind, Unity, Spiritual Science. They render to religious wisdom its due, but discard its divisiveness. They embrace the wisdom of Universal Spirituality to guide their lives.

These spiritual pioneers believe that Universal

Spirituality is a prize to be earned, not a dogma imposed by authority. They view all religions as an expression of evolutionary wisdom, but reject the claim that religious wisdom is an exclusive, denominational possession. They extend tolerance to all, even to the intolerant, and try to remove ignorance rather than punish it. They believe that the soul is the only permanent part of man and that the mind and body are its servants, gathering experience incarnation after incarnation, and refining it into spiritual wisdom. They regard death as a recurring incident in an endless life, thus radiating our existence with the optimistic grandeur of eternity.

It takes a strong will and an adventurous spirit to take up the quest for Universal Spirituality. The gates are open to the educated and the uneducated, rich and poor, religious and nonreligious. The spiritual explorers are alone, but not lonely. They are without the comfort of the majority's shared beliefs, but they are fulfilled with their keen sense of mission. Some, though reluctant to give up the sociability of their religions, are questioning their mythologies for historical certainties. Others have given up on religion and are seeking a new anchor to replace the one they left behind.

Practicing Universal Spirituality requires more than respectable church attendance. It calls for taking personal charge of communicating with God, rather than following a prescribed regimen created by others; avoiding cults, sects, and gurus; advancing evolution with our own spiritual exertion rather than relying on a future messiah for rewards.

Why does Universal Spirituality bring us closer to God than religiosity? Because religious petitionings, elaborate ceremonies, showy fanaticism, claims of special covenants, and charismatic leaders get between God and man.

They stir up intense feelings that lead to clashes between the sacredness of one religion and the holiness of another. Religiosity leads to a man-image God; Universal Spirituality penetrates to the God within us. That's why communicating with God in the privacy of our "closet" is more rewarding than participating in noisy ceremonials.

What raises Universal Spirituality above the din of religious certainties is the transcendent music of meta-physical thinking. In the nineteenth century, Ralph Waldo Emerson and Abraham Lincoln heard this meta-physical music and embraced it in preference to the pre-vailing religious practices. They were spiritual men in the universal sense of the word. In our own time, J. Krish-namurti, who melded the spiritual wisdom of the East and West, Alexander Solzhenitsyn, who came out of Russia's atheism, and Ernest Holmes, who illumined the spiritual law that undergirds all religions—all have pro-claimed that what the world needs is a spiritual renais-sance that's more vital than today's mainstream religions.

⌒○⌒

Universal Spirituality is not a new religion, a compilation of rules, or a status to be attained. It integrates the essence of religious wisdom but discards what is stultifying. It challenges us to transmute an anthropomorphic God that divides people, into a cosmic-energy God that unites them, but without losing the zeal of a personal God.

This may be difficult, because it takes much more imagination to picture Cosmic Energy as God than the man-made image of Him. But is it not logical to conjec-ture that cosmic and human energies are intertwined, having a dialogue? God is then no longer a foggy, invisible figure somewhere out there, but actually becomes a thinking Energy—a visible, breathing God animating and renewing our mind and body.

Universal Spirituality is not for armchair dilettantes. It dares its believers to test their new insights on the firing line of action. It has the power to jar and transmute egos from apathy to action. Its cosmic view opens vast opportunities for evolutionary progress. Allegiances become alliances.

Here is a transformation by one of its pioneers:

> I pledge allegiance to humanity
> And to the planet on which we live,
> One world, under God, indivisible,
> With peace and enlightenment for all.

It may take centuries before people will take personal charge of their spirituality, express it individually, and share it collectively without religious exclusivity. Universal Spirituality is still young. It struggles to survive, like a young sapling reaching for the sun while surrounded by shadows of old trees. But some day, far in the future, it will be fully grown, and the aged trees, having had their day, will fade away, and the new growth will take their place.

Chapter 3

An Evolutionary Concept

of God

I n this era of enormous technological and scientific advances, a group of leading spiritual scientists (Albert Einstein, David Bohm, Fritjof Capra, Rupert Sheldrake, and others) posit the theory, as a result of their spiritual and scientific research, that the universe is One Life, guiding the evolution of all its parts (organs) within the cosmos.

This "wholistic" vision, based on quantum physics, systemic biology, and cosmic energy, sets forth the proposition that ultimate particles of matter, such as electrons, are alive, endowed with consciousness and intelligence, and are reacting to their environment just as humans do. The spiritual scientists claim that all elements within the universe participate in the creative cosmic process, and they further assert that it behooves us to cooperate with the Cosmic Body (God), just as the organs cooperate in the human body.

I was privileged to attend a conference some twenty years ago in Ojai, California, where physicist David Bohm and J. Krishnamurti led a discussion on how physical science and spiritual consciousness meld into a cosmic energy grid that is the Universe God. Their revolutionary concept of an evolutionary God gripped my imagination. It challenged my biblical view, and in the years that followed I tried to visualize God not only as Cosmic Energy flowing through my mind/body, but also as a thinking Cosmic Intelligence that is always ready to engage my thoughts in a dialogue.

God is cosmic energy, guiding evolution with a cosmic wisdom that sustains everything within the universe. Air, water, fire are all cosmic energy. Minerals, plants, animals are cosmic energy. Man, consciousness, thinking, creating are cosmic energy. Galaxies, suns, planets are cosmic energy. Everything in the universe is cosmic energy. Nothing exists outside of cosmic energy.

What would happen to our concept of God if we discovered life on other planets? This would confuse and alarm creationists, just as the fact that the Earth orbits around the sun was a shocking discovery centuries ago. Mainstream religion would have to adjust, but this would most likely weaken the belief in Genesis and biblical history.

For those who view God as cosmic energy, there would be no problem. They would readily accept life in other parts of the cosmos as a natural phenomenon, an expansion of life in the process of cosmic creation. The spiritual universalists would view this as new confirmation of their vision of God, a God whose body is the boundless universe and within which all its entities (organs) are sustained by its inexhaustible cosmic energy.

I believe with the spiritual universalists that just as we have evolved out of the concept of many gods to one God, so finding life beyond Earth will evolve us from the Earth God of religion to the Cosmic God of evolution. It would lower denominational walls and focus our attention on what is outside those walls where, evolution works and man evolves.

Ever since the advent of the theory of evolution, science has gradually weakened the credibility of the idea of an apocalyptical transformation of humanity into a utopian state. But souls aflame with the messianic promise of paradise feel the presence of God more emotionally than do evolutionists, so the evolutionists' challenge is to experience God without the zealous emotion but with the same credence as the creationists do; to meld religion and science into the next stage of religious evolution—the concept of Universal Spirituality.

As the human species evolved, people created mythological gods, and in the process the worshipers advanced mankind. The power of myth, together with religious wisdom, has civilized millions and is still disciplining us today. Evolution has used the miracle of myth creatively with great success, but myth is no longer as believable as it was in the past. As a result, increasing numbers of former believers are thrown into a faithless vacuum, without guidance and without anything purposeful to live for.

Fortunately, however, evolution never stops functioning. It is guiding us out of the mythological age, just as it has successfully led us from many gods to one God. Many who have rejected a mythological God are now turning to a Cosmic Energy God. They find this more believable even though it is more difficult to envision than a man-image God. I believe the evolutionary Cosmic Energy God will supersede the man-image God and will bring humanity closer to a universal spirituality; but it will be a slow process.

If we could wave a wand and complete in one second a project that usually takes a year, would that be a blessing or a curse? A curse! Why? Because it would deprive us of the lessons gained from creative work. Compressing time unnaturally in growing food, building a home, or writing a book would be impeding evolution. The instant-result syndrome has given us Tums for upset stomach, aspirin for headache, alcohol for relaxation, coffee for quick-pick-me-ups, and dozens of other time-savers. But in rushing to squelch effects, we forget that if we would take time to look into causes, the knowledge of the causes could become our natural healing ally.

It seems logical that we should not rush time, but savor and enjoy it; that we are more in tune with the wisdom of the evolutionary process when we let time flow naturally than when we hurry it with a quick fix, quick buck, quick gratification, or quick anything.

It is interesting to compare the view held by the creationists that God created the Earth in six days, with the view of the evolutionists that the Earth has been evolving for four and a half-billion years. It is a profound contrast between the personal God who "hurried" Earth's creation and the evolutionary God that stretched it over billions of years.

What is the actual difference between a personal God and a Cosmic Energy God? In a profound sense, there is no difference. Both are reaching for the same God in different ways. Because of free will, it is natural that we should differ on the most challenging choice facing our lives, and it is understandable why the majority has chosen the personal approach to God. It simulates the warm, intimate human experience. It has worked successfully for ages and is still elevating millions from their lower to their higher human nature.

The evolutionary, cosmic-energy concept of God is more elusive, but it can give us the same warm feeling if we use our imagination to picture cosmic energy as an active, caring, and life-giving power that renews our mind and body.

The longings are the same; but the orthodox view rejects evolution in favor of living forever in heaven, while the cosmic-energy concept conjectures that each individual life (soul) is in a constant state of evolving.

It is the process of spiritual evolution that provides the means to transmute sinners into saints, and, again, it is a slow process. It takes a lot of evolving to reach a state of unselfishness, purity, and love. Just as it took eons to change simple forms into complex ones, so it may take countless lifetimes to transmute human nature into its highest state. That's why reincarnation is as convincing to me as the theory of evolution.

It took a lot of experiencing and suffering before the human species cleansed itself of bestiality, battle hunger, and lust. And it will take a lot more time before we rid ourselves of aggressiveness, cunning, and cruelty.

Why do some people become saints and others remain sinners? Because some learn to speed up their evolution by experimenting with idealistic goals, while others are content to stay on the treadmill of their lower human natures. Another plausible reason is that the sinner is a young soul that has experienced fewer incarnations than the saint. There is justice in evolution, and the more we understand its wisdom, the more we see how evolutionary justice works in our lives.

The operating law of evolution involves constant change, constant becoming, so that the myriad entities of the universe can evolve into grander forms and expanded consciousness. But because the human species is in no hurry to change its civilized human nature into a spiritual one, many millions still carry their savage propensities in their genes. The savage killed singly; civilized man kills collectively and on a bloodier scale. He has invented wonderful creature comforts but made little progress in distributing them fairly. He has sharpened his religious and ideological intellect but lacks the wisdom to contain its divisive violence. Evolution is telling us, in no uncertain terms, that we are barely out of the infant stage of our evolutionary development.

When human travail periodically reaches a critical mass, evolution comes to its rescue by regenerating us with a burst of new thinking. The Ten Commandments changed hordes of golden-calf nihilists into disciplined, God-fearing people. The Buddha's spiritual insight that intense desire was the principal cause of human suffering changed millions who followed his Four Noble Truths and Eightfold Path. Jesus' spiritual wisdom of "loving one another" filled millions of empty lives with faith and purpose.

Our civilization is reaching a critical point, but evolution is not neglecting us. It is calling our attention to Universal Spirituality, and an increasing number of enlightened people are beginning to practice what they understand of it. Will they hold back the raging tide of malevolence in our midst? Evolution will have its way.

Chapter 4

The Battle between the

Old and the New

Deep in the heart of man is a longing to live for something great. The yearning is linked to a Cosmic Intelligence, and the line of communication is always open. That's why a scoundrel, no matter how fragile his connection with the divine, can eventually become a saint.

But because the connection is invisible, many find it unbelievable. The scientific revolution has conditioned us to believe only in what we see, and that makes the unmarked path from the lower to our higher nature more difficult to see.

We began our civilizing Godward journey thousands of years ago with fetishes, sacrifices, and mythology. We refined it with religion, proselytized it with "holy" wars, and merchandized it with missionaries. Millions died because the leaders couldn't agree on how to transmute our religious longings into a brotherhood and sisterhood of humanity.

After centuries of violence, the major religions have solidified their gains, but the twenty-first century is threatening them from two diametrically opposed directions: the reawakening of fundamentalism and the growth of nihilism. Iran is the ominous example of one, the former Soviet Union of the other. Between these two extremes there is a slackening of dogma. People are changing from tighter to looser religions, but the walls between them are still intact. The era of relying on holy leaders for an interpretation of God is slowly ending, and people are seeing the logic of taking charge of their own spiritual development.

The following confrontation at a typical symposium is a microcosm of what is taking place, with many variations, in the Western world.

Arrayed against a rabbi, a priest, and a minister were three laypersons: a Jew, a Catholic, and a Protestant. The moderator was a young woman psychologist. Her lively, intelligent eyes roved over an audience of several hundred people.

The Jewish layperson, a suave-looking young man in his thirties, spoke first. He directed his remarks to the three clergymen, but particularly to the rabbi.

"Inspired reading material is now available to the masses. Formerly it was only available to the classes," he began. "By the classes I mean the learned clergy who told their followers what to believe and what not to believe. By reading and thinking beyond my religion, I've liberated myself from your dogmatisms. I find a greater challenge in discovering spiritual truth myself than in having it served up by tradition and digested by literalism."

"Do-it-yourself religious thinking may be all right for the few, but not for the many," replied the rabbi, who was wearing a yarmulke. "Without codifying the Jewish concept of God, individual religious effort would soon dissipate into a spiritless void, and Judaism with it. We must be practical, realistic. Most people will not take time to think for themselves. There are only a few like you. Our concern is for the many. They need our guidance, and we're not about to abdicate our duty to the millions of Jews for a few isolated ones like you."

"But if the few see something more vital than what is being prescribed for the many," the layman rebutted, "shouldn't we explore it rather than keep ourselves bottled up in Talmudic lore?"

"Who says it's more vital? It's only your opinion

against thirty-five hundred years of tradition," the rabbi shot back.

After several more heated exchanges, the moderator called on the Catholic layperson, an immaculately dressed young woman.

"Although we come from different religious backgrounds," she said, turning to the Jewish speaker who preceded her, "I have more in common with you than with my priest. Catholic fundamentalism has reached the end of a religious evolutionary cycle. We can no longer let its well-intentioned leaders do the thinking for us. New inspirational ideas are clamoring for our attention."

The Roman-collared priest on the dais immediately moved in on the discussion.

"With apologies to the rabbi, with whom I have more in common than with my Catholic rebel, I want to emphasize a very important point. Judaism's one-God concept would have remained a mere local discovery had it not been for us, who took it to the far corners of the earth. We turned heathens into God-loving people. We changed the course of history. After two thousand years of organizing and protecting our flock, we'd be derelict if we let our members wander aimlessly without our accumulated Catholic wisdom. If we did, there would be a wholesale return to the heathenism from which we sprang."

"Do I look like a heathen to you?" the Catholic lay person asked. "When I do my own thinking, I feel closer to God than when I let the Pope do my thinking."

"You may not look like a heathen, but without Catholic discipline, your children and your children's children would eventually be sucked into a spiritless void. I agree with the rabbi—the-do-it yourself self-proclaimed experts will not improve on the religious wisdom of the ages."

The moderator stopped the verbal fireworks and called on the Protestant layman, a hippie-yuppie hybrid whose long hair contrasted with his striped gray business suit.

"First," he began, "let me assure everybody in the audience that my two lay colleagues are not a couple of loose free-thinkers. On the contrary, they, like myself, are trying to practice a universal spirituality that requires more than mere church attendance. We're not satisfied with reaching for the Unknown through hymns and sermons. We want to experience God with all the pluralistic insights we can glean, from whatever source, and fashion them into a spiritual discipline that goes beyond adherence to rite and ceremony. We want to raise the moral quality of our lives, not because some church authority tells us to do it, but because we're convinced of it ourselves."

"Let's hear now," said the moderator politely, "what the Protestant minister has to say about all this."

The minister, not much older than his Protestant counterpart, rose from his seat and walked to the lectern. "The three rebels," he began, "have overlooked an important fact. Religions haven't stultified; they've been constantly reforming, revising, and loosening their dogmas. The Jews discovered, the Catholics merchandized, and the Protestants have refined the concept of God. To give up what we've learned for a do-it-yourself kind of religion would be like blotting out all we've learned about electricity and starting all over again. The falling away from organized religion has brought cynicism, despair, drugs, and a proliferation of cults in search of quick answers. I agree that religions need revitalizing, but let's do it within the time-tested truths, not according to the ideas of loners or guru-followers. A coal at the edge of a burning pile cools quickly. Within the pile, each coal receives heat from the other. On the outside, it becomes just a piece of cold carbon."

The ex-Protestant rose slowly. The minister had struck a cogent blow against individual religion. The audience waited eagerly for the reply.

"What if the burning pile accomplished nothing more than burning itself out into slag? Or worse, if the fire jumped and burned other piles into slag? You know what I mean: proselytizing."

The audience seemed to like the quick retort. The Protestant layman raced on. "I'm not for gurus or cults, nor for fooling around with shallow substitutes. What my colleagues and I are proposing is to let the full-grown religions die gracefully. Their cycle is over even as cycles of civilization are born, grow old, and die. New buds are forming everywhere to unite the world into what Teilhard de Chardin calls a new global theosphere, a common spirituality. New spiritual shoots are growing, inspiring new ideas about God. For instance, we no longer regard sin as an act deserving the old biblical fire-and-brimstone punishment, but as a foolish mistake that may ruin our life. I could cite other examples."

The moderator got up from her chair. "This is a good note on which to end the panelists' discussion. Now, ladies and gentlemen, you may ask questions from the floor."

A well-groomed, middle-aged woman a—typical parishioner of the kind you would expect to find in a fashionable Episcopalian church—walked to the microphone and in a deliberate, articulate voice put this question to the three laypersons:

"Despite religious divisiveness, you will have to admit there is discipline within each denomination, especially where it is needed among the uneducated. What makes you think that loosening these organizational bonds into unorganized personal thinking will not degenerate into a babel of subjective chaos? Dare we gamble our mature stability for the upheavals of the Moonies, Hare Krishnas, and the do-it-yourself wanderers who are getting into drugs, free love, and suicide? Dare we tinker with something that has worked, that has civilized the world?"

The Jewish layperson was the first to respond. "Why not gamble with the new? The situation we've inherited has created centuries of prejudice and violence. At the tip of change there is always discord. We must risk the discord, the gurus, the cults, the aimless wanderers. But they will disappear, and the restless searchers will eventually find their answers in self-disciplined, universal spirituality."

The Catholic layperson gave a short answer. "We have too many religious leaners, and not enough spiritual lifters. By lifting, I mean more personal effort to reach for God than leaning on church attendance."

The Protestant layperson was just as succinct. "Whether we like it or not, the flow from organized to personal religion is gaining momentum. Solzhenitsyn's hope for a global spiritual renaissance, and Teilhard de Chardin's forecast of a spiritual mutation, are harbingers of the change we're talking about."

The meeting came to an end.

To talk idealism is easy; to live it is difficult. But without groping for plausible assumptions, there would be little civilizing progress. The most noble conjecture we can make is that somehow, some way, we are linked to a

31

Cosmic Intelligence. The yearning to link up with it is the history of mankind's spiritual evolution.

Spiritual imagination, tempered by prudence, is the gateway to the unknown. If we dream, let it be a noble dream, one that links us to a Cosmic God—a vast and mighty energy without bounds. Only by dreaming do we awaken our awareness that we are part of a grand universe, one in which we play a prominent role.

Chapter **5**

Spirituality, Morality,

Science, Intellect, and

Human Nature

Spirituality is intuitive and inspirational. It is beyond being smart, intelligent, and wise. It is a partnership with God, where we receive cosmic energy to keep us alive, and we in turn use human energy to advance mankind.

Eastern wisdom describes the essence of spirituality in terms of what it is not. Krishnamurti has proclaimed this provocatively:

Devotion: The sages of the ages apotheosized it, the world's scriptures glorified it. Yet devotion, followed to its logical conclusion, ends up a vice because intense dedication to an "ism" leads to propaganda, proselytizing, and violence.

Holiness: A virtue? No! Look at the havoc it causes as the holiness of one religion clashes with the sacredness of another.

Loyalty: A virtue? No! Intense loyalty to one religion screens out what is good in other religions. Martyrdom is loyalty gone amok.

Traditionalism: A great virtue? Not if a stultifying conformity to tradition prevents inquiry. Being bound to the past can stunt creative impulses. Traditionalism dulls and then clamps the mind in a vise.

Does this make sense? The clergy will ridicule it. The secularists will shrug it off as impractical. Yet there is a haunting ring of truth in what this spiritual sage, Krishnamurti, says, even though it goes against commonly accepted beliefs. Devotion, holiness, loyalty, tradition have taken centuries to evolve and have elevated mankind's thinking. But what Krishnamurti sees in these virtues is a hankering for the sacred religious past which, in his view, poisons the living present.

Morality and Spirituality

Morality is a logical, man-made view of values to under-pin a good life and is given authenticity by sacred scriptures. Moses' Ten Commandments constituted a primer needed to create a moral environment, and it was validated by a command from God.

The nature of morality differs with every religion, culture, and region. Polygamy is moral among the Muslims but not among Jews and Christians. Morality changes with the times. Human sacrifice was moral among the heathens, but not when they evolved into civilized nations. Slavery was moral in America as late as 1860, but not today. Slaughtering animals in prescribed ways to celebrate religious holidays is moral among Jews and Christians, but not for Buddhists or for an increasing number of vegetarians. Morals differ among Eskimos, Africans, Indian tribes, and generally among Eastern and Western cultures. They differ less among developed nations where they have been universalized to similar standards.

In contrast to the changing nature of morality, spirituality is a universal value that transforms lives in visible ways. It mutes anger, lust, greed, pride, and a host of other moral flaws, and it promotes the character-building traits of kindness, unselfishness, and compassion.

Science and Spirituality

Physical science deals with predictable matter (energy), which is observable and measurable. Spiritual science deals with the less measurable and predictable will, emotions, and thought, as well as the purpose of our existence. Physical science does not ask the meaning of existence. It is content to understand the natural laws relating to how matter is made, how it works, and how it behaves.

The whys and wherefores of our existence belong to spiritual science, which must also study the subject of thought—a subtle energy that is as elusive as the wind. Thought cannot be studied as a physical science because it does not lend itself to controlled experimentation. How can we measure sublime inspiration, deep depression, freakish behavior, or what goes on the minds of people of different cultures?

Yet it is not far-fetched to postulate that thoughts "talk" to the body's molecules, and that what they say affects the body in many visible ways. For many people, relying on healing thoughts often works more effectively than doctors' prescriptive medicines.

Thoughts move molecules in different configurations that either heal or hurt. The fact that those who can picture healing cosmic energy flowing through their bodies can reverse their physical and mental maladies is proof that molecules respond to thoughts. Thousands of such healings have been documented in many countries.

Students who are knowledgeable in the science of thought, especially those who have studied *Science and Health,* by Mary Baker Eddy, believe that just as divine thought can heal, so mortal thoughts can hurt. Angry and anxious laden thoughts can arrange molecules in ways that sag the body and confuse the mind. Thoughts have the power to kill and to heal.

There are few mean people in their eighties and nineties. Most of them are kind and gracious. Might it not be proof that kind thoughts are a divine prescription for longevity?

Science is wonder; spirituality is wisdom. When the wonders of science reach an uncrossable border, wonder turns to spiritual wisdom. After years of exploring the limitless hidden laws of nature, Albert Einstein and other well-known scientists changed from wonder to cosmic spiritual wisdom. They proclaimed that their noblest motive for continuing scientific research was to explore inner man as well as the outer universe.

For most scientists, the search for coherent laws ends in equations. For the spiritual scientist, equations are not enough. Their quest for material knowledge is bound up with what it will do to enrich the soul, to mesh the microcosm with the macrocosm, the observer with the observed.

The spiritual scientists do not negate mainstream religion, but their reverence for God penetrates deeper than biblical absolutes; it is more in tune with open-ended Universal Spirituality. Scientists who are enchanted only with the spectacular space stations, global communications, and technological achievements experience the excitement of the unprecedented, but not the extradimensional fulfillment of transcendence.

Because scientists have become as pivotal to our times as the Prophets were in theirs, it is essential that science should fuse wonder with wisdom and materialism with spirituality, and blaze a new trail to God

Intellect and Spirituality

Intellect is limited to reason, and it is prone to sway from beneficent rational thinking to irrational thinking that can manipulate mankind into mindless ideological and religious wars.

Without a spiritual overview to soften hard intellect, barren existential reason can draw us into stark pessimism. Sartre's lament "It is meaningless that we live and meaningless that we die" echoes this observation. Weakened by anger, depression, or self-pity, the realists who rely only on reason flay away at life's uncertainties until they fatigue their minds into despair. They are like the bee that hurls itself against a windowpane until it dies of exhaustion instead of saving itself by going back the way it came. Fighting uncertainties with mere reason leaves us in a dark place of ignorance.

But if intellect can make room for an understanding of spirituality, we will be able to develop a bird's-eye view from which to study and shed light on our problems. As we grow in spirituality, frustrating resistance changes to detached acceptance, relaxation replaces anxiety, pessimism turns into optimism, despair is infused with the oxygen of hope. It is a dynamic intervention of the cosmic spirit, a more powerful healing agent than any depression pill conceived by medical science.

It is easy to see the difference between a man of intellect and one who uses intellect in combination with spirituality. The former shows it in his eager-beaver behavior whether he's palpitating for success, glorifying religion, or pushing a political ideology. There is no visible empathetic glow, only ambitious striving for results and rewards. The spiritual man uses reason to function on the secular level, but with an introspective vision that glows visibly with serene poise and vibrant vitality. Combining intellect with spirituality is the ideal balance for adventurous evolution.

Human Nature and Spirituality

Unfortunately, human nature is slow to change, and practicing spirituality requires changing some of our deeply entrenched human habits and attitudes. For instance, we need to change from opinionating to observing, from panting for revenge to forgiving, from relative to absolute honesty, from nonstop busyness to daily periods of meditation, from egoism to self-effacement, from desire for certainly to being content with uncertainty.

A lawyer, a doctor, and a businessman—friends with whom I lunch occasionally— tried to explain to me why it is foolish to hope for human nature to change.

Said the lawyer: "Human nature can't be changed! Accept things as they are, George—mostly rotten—and forget your universal spirituality."

Said the doctor: "It's all in the genes. If you're programmed to be a scoundrel, that's the way you'll grow up. Oh, you may delude yourself and think you're changing, but your genes keep the character mold the way an acorn molds the tree. Trying to change human nature is like trying to grab a ray of light, George: it can't be done."

Said the businessman: "Look back a few thousand years. King David sent his friend into battle so he could have his wife. That's human nature for you, even in the best of men. It's persisted throughout civilization. It may change a trifle here and there, but deep down it remains the same: selfish, unchangeable."

The world isn't changing because good men like these aren't changing. But just as humanity has evolved from heathenism to civilization, so ordinary human nature will eventually evolve into spiritual nature. The souls of the human species are young. As they grow older, in future incarnations, they will transmute their human experiences into universal spiritual wisdom. Evolution will prevail.

Chapter 6

Meditation and the Soul

The soul is not an impersonal abstraction; it is the active intermediary between cosmic creation and the human ego. The soul needs human experience to evolve, while the ego needs the soul's guidance to make evolutionary progress a reciprocal relationship. This reciprocity between the ego and the soul is the active communication that propels evolution. When we are listening for guidance during quiet times, we are listening to all our past incarnational experience—the accumulated wisdom of the soul.

It is reasonable to believe that when we seek God's guidance during meditation, the soul is activated, and the selfish ego thoughts lose their power as nobler ones take their place. And on the physical level, the body actually relaxes when the soul responds to our quest for counseling.

Often I find that describing an insight in the first person is more convincing than in an expository manner. My soul is the link between God and me. Acting as an intermediary during meditation, my soul can convey insights from God more directly than through noisy ceremonials. I find that listening for insights during quiet times personalizes my connection with God more intimately than when I was in orthodox Judaism, participating in the rite of public petitioning.

The first step in preparation for receiving inspiring insights is to assume that our human mind is rooted in Cosmic Energy (God). Without that assumption, we have only our intellect to rely on, and it can only offer valuable secular ideas, not intuitional wisdom beyond reason.

The second step is to create an orderly mind. Unless it is cleared of aimless thoughts that roam at will, the mindscape will be cluttered with attention robbing debris that will prevent putting up an antenna to pick up spiritual intuitions. And if we are really serious about receiving messages from beyond reason, the body also needs to be kept clean, preferably with vegetarian food.

The third step is to quiet the mind for a half-hour a day and listen to God's guidance. I have rarely received an insight for a creative real-estate venture, or an idea for my writing, while I was on the run pursuing secular interests. When thoughts appeared on my mind's screen during quiet time-meditation, I knew that the elevating ones came from the wisdom of Cosmic Energy, while the ordinary ones were from my reasoning human brain. It was at the urging of my cosmic thoughts that I made one of my most important life decisions: that Universal Spirituality was the next progressive, evolutionary step for me—beyond the wisdom of traditional religions.

When I seek guidance from God's silence, I receive responses that are more elevating, more reliable than the advice I get from my peers. Although I enjoy their companionship and friendship, I rarely rely on their counsel. Most of my decisions originate during quiet-time "conversing" with the Cosmic Energy (God). It speaks to me with greater authority and clarity than the opinions of my fellow man. Daily quiet time, reflection, and reading spiritual literature are the most reliable guides for a fulfilling life.

The goal in quiet-time meditation is to merge our human awareness with the Cosmic Awareness. This is also the goal of the mystic. To prepare for this, he enters a state of moral and spiritual purification until he rises above the din of the senses to a place where subject and object blend. He does not dissolve the ego psychologically, but he keeps it secondary to his higher state of consciousness.

He functions effortlessly with calm composure.

On the secular plane, the mystic demonstrates the repatterning of his life with clarity of mind, with intuitive perceptiveness, superior judgment, and unusual skill in whatever practical work he chooses for a livelihood. He engages in his worldly work with interest, cheerfulness, and intelligence. He is tolerant of others; he understands their cultural conditioning of "me against them," but he does not confront them with it.

This mix of dedication, detachment, and practicality is characteristic of people who experience God more profoundly than those with closed religious systems that rely on prescribed rules and beliefs.

In my efforts to practice what I understand of spirituality, I have formulated a four-way plan involving meditation, evaluation, transformation, and implementation.

During meditation I evaluate any new insight that challenges an old one. After days, weeks, or months of letting it bubble in my mind, if it continues to prod me to change, I'll make the mental transformation and follow it up with the physical implementation. Implementation is the key for transforming a new thought into action.

If we are serious about self-enlightenment, we will tend to our secular obligations but set aside a half-hour of quiet time each day to meditate. This is when God talks to us through the soul in the form of transcendental thoughts. We need not be scholars or theologians to explore ideas such as: Where did we come from, and where are we going? What is the source of our breathing and thinking energy? Why is there so much human suffering? What happens to life after death? Is reincarnation a valid theory? Thoughts like these mined during quiet times do not have final answers, but they promote the growth of Universal Spirituality. Once a seed of spirituality is planted, it attracts insights to fertilize its growth.

One such insight that came to me is the difference between WHO I am and WHAT I am. It is like comparing the wave with the ocean. The wave is *who* I am; the ocean is *what* I am. Thus all the attributes of the finite (wave) are contained in the infinite (ocean). Who I am is transitory: my physical body; what I am is eternal: my soul, the real me.

Of the various theories about the soul and life after death, the most convincing one, to me, was put forth by the prominent theosophical student of the Unknown, C. F. Leadbeater. Writing about a hundred years ago, he explored the principles of Universal Spirituality, evolution, reincarnation, and karma. He was also a most intuitive student of clairvoyance as it related to life after death. The following is a concise overview of his book *Life after Death*:

The astral (emotional) and the mental (thinking) bodies interpenetrate the physical body, and upon death the soul, with its astral and mental atoms, separates from the physical and continues its existence.

On the astral plane, the undisciplined person leads a disturbed type of existence, as he or she had on the physical plane, or as in a bad dream. The more evolved person leads an emotionally stable life as he or she did on the physical level. Eventually, the astral-body atoms die, and the soul functions on the mental plane.

Life on the mental level is lived on two tiers: the lower level, where those who have done little creative thinking on the physical plane experience an ordinary existence, and the higher mental level, where those who have applied their minds creatively enjoy a more interesting mental life.

After digesting experiences on the astral and mental planes, the soul is ready for another physical life, taking along the lessons learned during the last physical, astral, and mental existences—a sort of computer printout of the past and its accumulated learned lessons.

These thoughts naturally lead us to a discussion of reincarnation: is it fact or fantasy?

Chapter 7

Reincarnation:

Fact or Fantasy?

What is our destiny? Where are we going? The conjectures range from the vague speculations of nihilistic philosophers to the heavenly certainties of the religious clergy. There is, however, a plausible hypothesis between these two extremes. It is reincarnation—a radiant, open-ended view of life which proposes that we are evolving and traveling on a never-ending evolutionary journey resonating with the grandeur of immortal adventure.

It seems to me the height of pessimistic, unscientific reasoning to believe that where we are is the end of our evolution. It is a scientific fact that matter and energy are interchangeable; that neither is ever destroyed. Then isn't it equally conceivable that the "I"-consciousness energy, the soul, doesn't suffer oblivion either? If matter is imperishable, why isn't individualized awareness, a higher form of energy, also imperishable?

The intuitive wisdom of the Prophets, the grand perceptions of an Einstein, a Gandhi, or a Goethe, could not have evolved in one lifetime. A more reasonable explanation is that their insights were the accumulated memories forged during previous lifetimes. How else can we explain child prodigies effortlessly mastering higher mathematics or difficult musical scores, while others exposed to the same opportunities can't learn them in an entire lifetime?

Skeptics contend that there is no proof of reincarnation since, we don't remember any of our past lives. The answer to this objection is that evolution is wise and merciful. Instead of clogging our memories with details of past lives, we inherit only the distilled propensities of skills, capacities, and values we learned in previous incarnations. Occasionally, memories do come through. Dr.

Ian Stevenson has described a number of authentic past-life recall cases in his book *Twenty Cases Suggestive of Reincarnation.*

Reincarnation is accepted as a fact among millions of Hindus and as a prudent conjecture among many-well known Western thinkers, Ralph Waldo Emerson, Benjamin Franklin, and Thomas Edison among them. Whether we feel the validity of reincarnation intuitively or accept it on the basis of logical thinking, it charges our lives with a vibrancy that only a belief in deathlessness can bring.

Since man's experiences have been nurtured on personal attachments, it's not surprising that life after death has become the ultimate attachment. For fundamentalists, living in heaven forever is the central certainty; for agnostics it's a "maybe"; and for atheists, oblivion is the answer. It is understandable that since people differ on lesser uncertainties, they should differ most emphatically on what happens after death.

My limited personal view of immortality, based on the theory of reincarnation, assumes that the real me is not my body, but my soul. It refines by body's human experiences into insights to guide my evolution. My present brain does not remember the details of lessons learned during past incarnations, but my soul does in the form of general proclivities acquired from past experiences. And the lessons learned during my present life will be carried over by my soul into the next.

Just as a seed falls to the ground where soil, water, and air give it another round of life, so the soul—the permanent atom somewhere in the atmosphere—seeking another incarnation, finds the sperm of man and the egg of woman to give it another round of physical existence. And just as the seed carries within it the information to grow into a particular tree or bush, so the soul, carrying within it the proclivities of previous incarnations, evolves into the person who inherits the characteristics of the soul's accumulated information.

Obviously, this assumption can't be proved scientifically; but this kind of thinking edges us closer to making new tracks on the pathless Unknown.

I feel comfortable with the concept that life is a never-ending destiny, not a static stopping-place in heaven. I do not claim this as a certainty; but among the many uncertainties about life after death, reincarnation of the soul seems the most plausible. And because it is tied to the wisdom of evolution, my belief increases as my soul travels on its immortal journey into eternity.

Reincarnation has been integrated in the East as a faith of continuing life. The West still views it with considerable skepticism. Here are some examples of Western reactions to the idea:

A church-going woman: "Reincarnation does not square with the Bible. I believe in a God in heaven who will decide what happens to me when I get there."

A loquacious atheist: "Reincarnation is a lot of poppy-cock; the same kind of wild imagining that's in the Bible."

A religious agnostic: "I hope there's no such thing as reincarnation, because I wouldn't want to come back to struggle for another lifetime in this crazy world."

One with a vague knowledge about reincarnation: "I don't like the idea because I wouldn't want to come back as a bug or an animal." (Of course, this is a wrong view, because the human being does not reincarnate into a lower species.)

A Jesuit priest said that he was sure he would be resurrected at Jesus' second coming and live forever in afterlife bliss. A rabbi said, with a vague wave of the hand, "God knows; I don't." This roughly sums up mainstream beliefs about life after death in the Judeo-Christian tradition.

An informed reincarnationist puts it this way:

"Reincarnation takes us into eternity with the assurance of immortality. It's a glorious evolutionary journey involving eons of adventurous lifetimes."

A reincarnationist friend of mine described the essence of his belief about eternity in these terse sentences:

"I'm eighty-four years old. My body is used up. My soul is eager for more evolutionary experiences, for a new beginning in a new incarnation. While my body is weak, my mind is alive with anticipation for my next life. Where will I be born? What will I do? I know that what I've learned in this life I'll use in the next. I'm grateful to the wisdom of evolution for providing new adventures in the endless lives ahead of me."

We have no hard evidence for the beliefs of the priest, the rabbi, or the reincarnationist. All we can do is speculate. Even though I was conditioned in my early years by Judaic beliefs, I choose the concept of reincarnation because the validity of evolution seems more credible than my former literal orthodox faith. This is what I believe now. However, I hope my mind won't be closed to any new epochal idea as my soul keeps probing the cosmic silence in this and future incarnations.

Chapter 8

The Malevolent Threats

to Our Culture

I t's obvious that there's a cultural war going on between the malevolence that is threatening to engulf us and the benevolent efforts of those who are trying to halt the avalanche of dangers.

Global Pollution

The Earth is as aware of what is going on within its sphere of life as we are of what is happening in our bodies. It is kept alive by cosmic energy the same way we are. Just as our body knows how to coagulate blood, change food into energy, maintain body temperature, and perform hundreds of complex tasks to keep it alive, so the Earth maintains the right balance of chemicals, controls its temperatures, and regulates countless conditions to renew itself. Perhaps it even creates ice ages to cool its fever; and it uses marvelous skills to protect itself from the sun so it doesn't scorch its living parts.

However, man's pollutions are making the Earth ill, just as microbes in our bodies make us ill. But the Earth is far more resilient and resourceful than we are, so we are more likely to destroy ourselves by wounding the Earth than we are to endanger its continuity. We can't survive without its nourishment; it can survive without us.

But can we survive if the malevolent influences that are corroding our society continue to grow? The following is a partial list of the social problems that must be solved.

The Proliferation of Deadly Weapons

The dark side of technology has let escape the deadliest genie ever conceived: nuclear bombs, poison gas, and an array of deadly weapons that can kill thousands in seconds. And we don't have the will or the wisdom to put it back into the bottle. These weapons are potentially as destructive as whatever happened millions of years ago when an asteroid smashed into the Earth. Political maneuvering will not halt the genie's collision with catastrophe; only an idea as culture-changing as Universal Spirituality can eradicate the genie before it eradicates us.

Religious Zealotry

It's ironic, and the height of incongruity, that the most fervent devotees of God often become the most dangerous members of society. They revere the promises of heaven more than the lives of people on Earth. Their zealous religious thinking, backed by emotional rhetoric, has slaughtered millions. These hotheads are still among us—smart, intelligent, but not wise, and certainly not spiritual. Their followers love them, but the zealots corrupt this love by persuading their flocks to hate others. The Middle East is a bloody example of this incendiary thinking, as are many other areas on Earth.

Teenage Pregnancies

An increasing number of teenagers are giving birth to unwanted children who will have little chance for a stable family environment and will more than likely become dysfunctional adults. Gone is the fragrance of romance and the disciplined courtship that elevated sex to the accompaniment of love. Too many teenagers today are more familiar with indiscriminate instant-gratification sex than with the waiting and mating game of enduring love. If the percentage of children born out of wedlock grows, we will probably see an increase of poverty and crime. All the preaching about family values will be of no avail unless a powerful idea, laden with hope and optimism, replaces the present teenage and young-adult slide into hopeless, rudderless lives.

The Private Possession of Guns

If the founding fathers could have foreseen today's proliferation of guns in the hands of undisciplined youth who are randomly killing hundreds of innocent people, they would have radically modified their declaration of the right to bear arms. It is ironic that we spend millions curtailing drugs, but allow the more lethal menace to legally multiply unabated. The law-abiding citizens are locked between an unholy alliance of an organized, well intentioned minority (NRA) and young ruffians who can procure a gun as easily as buying a pack of cigarettes. It is time to wake up and work toward a gunless society.

Drug, Alcohol, and Tobacco Addictions

With every breath we take, we're renewing our mind and body. Drugs, alcohol, and tobacco obstruct this natural flow of cosmic energy and debilitate mind and body. Many adjust and endure their addictions, a few get out of their dependencies, but the vast majority become a double problem: they slowly self-destruct, and in the process they become a burden to society—dependent leaners instead of contributing lifters.

The Normalizing of Gambling

Twenty-five hundred years ago, Aristotle said that man was made for work. It's still the most effective formula for wholesome living. But his sage advice is being flouted by a huge segment of our population that is encouraged to get something for nothing—the gambling mania. It extracts five hundred billion dollars a year, mainly from the pockets of the poor and the middle class.

Today government, which used to jail people for gambling, is itself sponsoring lotteries and licensing gambling on a scale that was unthinkable forty years ago. For many, betting to get much for little has become the American dream a corruption of the work ethic. Gambling is a leech that sucks money, along with morality, out of people who are blind to the harm it does to themselves and to society. It debases the lives of the gamblers and breaks up marriages and families.

Pornography

This four-billion-dollar-a-year industry is poisoning impressionable young minds and degrading sexuality for adults. It devalues romance, changes the thrill of a touch to a promiscuous clutch, and turns courtship into lust. It cheapens the most intimate and sacred communication between man and woman, thereby undermining healthy sexual expression in marriage and weakening family values.

Violent Entertainment

We absorb what we see, hear, and read. These things become ingrained in our psyche and the subconscious, affecting the way we think, speak, and act down to the most mundane mannerisms. Our own common sense should convince us that emulation is one of our natural traits. But the hustlers of violent entertainment don't care a whit about the harm it does to its viewers. With their love of money and their ability to manipulate the First Amendment with the best legal brains money can buy, they rake in enormous profits. They are as adept in mesmerizing us with seductive public relations as they are in corrupting our youth with violent entertainment.

Even children are constantly exposed to violence in TV programs, movies, and videos. This has the effect of making them callous instead of compassionate and gives them the idea that violence is the way to solve life's problems. In recent outbreaks of random violence in public schools, there was definite evidence that the young perpetrators were strongly influenced by video "games" and a motion picture titled *Born to Kill.* The situation is more than alarming, because the hustlers' appetite for profit is increasing, and so is the proliferation of guns—a lose-lose combination.

Gangs

To substitute for family life, the "lost" young are forming prowling packs just as tribes did in primitive times. To fill the vacuum of empty hours, they do what comes naturally to valueless lives: they concoct juvenile rules and live and die by them. They have no family guidance, no useful work, no purpose into which to channel their energies. While we should not hold them blameless for their wantonly destructive acts, neither should we hold ourselves blameless for not devising ways to steer them away from sinking into the quagmire of self-destruction.

Credit-Card Gouging

The credit-card idea is a great convenience for those who can afford to pay their bills on time. It is, however, a nightmare for the meager earners who are given easy access to the cards, buy beyond their means, and then get hooked on 18-percent interest rates. Many are eventually hounded into bankruptcy. Being constantly in debt beyond one's means is as deadly a virus as having a chronic physical malady. And this economic sickness will continue as long as the corporate money-lovers see the potential of huge profits by preying on the weaknesses of those who want more than they can afford. Free enterprise is wonderful—the best of all economic systems—but the plastic card is a marvelous innovation, only for the rich to become richer and the poor poorer.

The Vulgarizing of Our Language

The vulgar language in TV talk shows, movies, books, and rap music is seeping into our speech and cheapening human discourse. This insidious influence is thriving in sensational news and public parlance, and when it is drummed into our psyches on a daily basis, we begin to accept it as normal. A generation ago, only a small segment of the population indulged in coarse conversation, but today one hears the name-calling, the four-letter words, and the cheap talk not only in bars but in workplaces, at sporting events, and even in politics with increasing frequency. The acid-tongue lingo is worming its way into our culture, demeaning the art of polite conversation and courteous public parlance.

Terrorism

This is a new species of threat that is raising its venomous head. Less than a century ago, terrorists struck with guns or knives, one on one. Today they strike with bombs and kill hundreds at a time. And with the availability of nuclear weapons and poison gas, terrorism poses a staggering menace. This new threat may spread as religious, ethnic, and ideological leaders fail to reconcile their differences in ways that respect and meet each others' needs. Terrorism was born in the dark womb of technology—a treacherous monster whose madness is difficult to eradicate, because it combines deranged individuals and access to weapons of mass destruction.

The Dark Cloud of Global Communication

Technology has surged far ahead of spiritual wisdom. The speed of global communication is making information easily accessible to more people. But the power to disseminate world knowledge is gravitating into the hands of international businessmen who are more interested in profit than in human welfare. We know what happened in Russia when knowledge and power were centralized.

Democracy will weaken and slide into international commercial fascism unless spiritual wisdom is combined with
the boon of global communication. We need enlightened
economic leaders who put the welfare of people ahead of
profit, instead of the other way around.

Chapter **9**

Benevolent Solutions

Adding a Fourth R to Education

There is no short-range solution to these problems, but there is a long-range solution that will win the cultural war. Just as the freedom fighters years ago laid the foundation for the freedoms we enjoy today, so we should emulate them and initiate a long-range plan to raise the quality of life for future generations to enjoy.

In essence, we must improve education by adding universal spiritual wisdom as the fourth R to the required curriculum of the three R's—Reading, Writing, and 'Rithmatic. It should be taught in every classroom from the first grade through college, attuning the contents to each age. This would not be in opposition to those who believe in the separation of church and state because Universal Spirituality deals with how to find something big to live for, and how to reconcile differences between the nations of the world. It will infuse the values of cooperation and tolerance into the thinking of children during their formative years and inspire future adult generations to practice what they were taught.

The time to begin this major shift in the educational process is NOW. With a combination of private and public funds, from liberals as well as conservatives, we should recruit several thousand men and women versed in universal spirituality to teach their wisdom to the thousands of teachers who are already in the profession and to those who are studying to make teaching their career. This number should be increased each year until all teachers from the first grade on through college will be spiritually educated to inspire their students with the fourth "R" spelled *Universal Spiritual Wisdom*. They will teach their students that a life, like a three-legged table, will wobble without the fourth "R." They will use Einstein's logic that religion without science is blind, and science without spiritual wisdom is lame.

It's a visionary plan, but so was the vision of the freedom fighters. We can start now and give to posterity what the pioneer fighters gave to us.

Work—the Key to Social Order

The mark of enlightened capitalism is an economy in which private enterprise provides the bulk of employment, and the government provides work for those whom private enterprise can't absorb. It's a win-win-win plan, because it strengthens private enterprise, provides work for the unemployed, and reduces crime.

President Franklin Roosevelt solved the youth unemployment problem with the creation of the Civilian Conservation Corps (CCC). It put the unemployed to work, shoring up the country's infrastructure by repairing roads and bridges, building parks, and working at various other needed projects.

Today the CCC is needed more than ever, not only to repair our decaying infrastructure, but to clear our streets of crime and to give hope to our unemployed, including the gangs that roam our streets. A modern CCC program would pay a minimum hourly wage, provide housing in barracks now being vacated by our armed forces, and include meaningful recreational activities. The training and work involved would make it possible for many to eventually enter the mainstream of private business.

Help from Religions, Civic Groups, and Others

It is obvious that we have many problems to solve in order to achieve the goal of a morally healthy culture. Fortunately, good people far outnumber the bad. That's our main advantage in the looming conflict between the malevolent and benevolent influences in our society. There are a number of religious, civic, and other groups that could be recruited to help accelerate the process of making Universal Spirituality a working reality in human affairs.

Fundamentalists

Fundamentalists are evangelists with a thicker layer of zealous certainties. Their family values are exemplary, but their virtues are smothered by a suffocating self-righteousness. However, evolution is a patient guide. Fundamentalists are good people, with the potential to transmute their intense love for an exclusive God into an *inclusive* one.

Mainstream Religionists

Churchgoers are a sturdy stock of people, well equipped morally to change conditions in society. They are the footsoldiers who will eventually evolve from religious wisdom to Universal Spirituality—the most formidable weapon against all kinds of malevolence.

The Baha'is

The Baha'is believe that the primary challenge in dealing with the world's travail is to add a spiritual dimension to secular problems. They believe in the wholeness of the universe and the brotherhood of the human race. When all the diverse parts learn to cooperate it will eventually lead to world government, international law, and world peace.

Promise-Keepers

Throughout history, new shoots have sprung from mainstream religions. One such is the Promise-Keepers. Close to a million men meet each year in various stadiums around the country to revitalize their fidelity to their wives and children. The central idea is to strengthen family values. These are good, moral men, but their belief that man can be perfected only by accepting Christ as his redeemer regrettably separates them from Buddhists, Jews, Muslims, and others. When this is overcome and all religions are invited to join forces to advance family values, there will be more Promise-Keepers in attendance to make more people aware that when the family crumbles, civilization crumbles.

Ethical Humanists

These people rely on their intellect to guide their lives, and they do an excellent job of it. They are often in leadership positions in their communities. Having found organized religion wanting, they have embraced reason as a substitute. However, they are bound to find bare reason just as deficient. When their restless natures begin probing for something new, they will discover Universal Spirituality and use it in creative ways to confront the malevolent influences at work in our society.

Enlightened Employers and Employees

Employers and employees comprise the majority of our population. The roles they play will determine to a great extent the outcome of today's social conflicts. The ideal economic system would be a partnership between the employers and employees, where each cares for the needs of the other, and together they produce goods that contribute to the welfare of society. Such an economic structure would change capitalism from worshiping profit to serving people. Signs of such enlightened entrepreneurship are appearing in many places and in many forms. Businesses large and small are participating with various pro bono groups to provide food, clothing, and shelter for the needy; improving services and benefits for their customers; sharing profits and granting bonuses to their employees; caring for the safety, health, and environment of their workers and their families.

Judges, Lawyers, Policemen, Prison Wardens

Our judicial system protects our safety and freedom. It is the cohesive glue of law and order. Without its services we would be living in a social jungle. I am more appreciative than most Americans for its protection because of my personal experiences as a child living in the aftermath of the 1917 Russian revolution. Robbers pillaged and killed at will, and there were no police to call, nor lawyers or judges to process complaints. I tell my friends who grumble at some of the problems with our justice system that we're living in a law-and-order paradise compared to what I lived through and what is still happening in many other countries. The judges, lawyers, police, and prison wardens who are protecting our safety and freedom play leading roles in providing a safe environment for Universal Spirituality to take root and grow into a more benevolent society.

Rotarians, Kiwanians, Lions, et al.

Civic groups make tremendous contributions to the welfare of society. Among the leading ones are the Rotarians, Kiwanians, and Lions. I've been a Rotarian for thirty-eight years and have mingled with many Kiwanians and Lions. There's as much enthusiasm among these civic groups for helping people as there is among churchmen, with the added bonus that civic help crosses ethnic, racial, and religious boundaries. On the local level, these clubs throughout the world initiate and shore up existing programs involving social agencies, schools, health clinics, libraries, and cultural centers. They feed the poor, and when a glaring need arises in their communities, they are among the first to meet it. I attended an international convention of Rotarians some years ago in Denver. The obvious camaraderie of people from over a hundred countries and from every major culture, race, and religion was an inspiring exhibition of universal fellowship, a shining example for different religions to emulate.

Spiritual Scientists

The scientific geniuses who have given us electricity, modern transportation, medical advances, abundant food, and dozens of creature comforts are playing as significant a role in our lives as those who inspire us with wisdom. Each contribution complements the other. The spiritual scientists see cosmic energy as alive with awareness, purpose, and intelligence— a creative force that communicates with us more intimately than we realize. Combining their scientific research with spiritual insights, they will be among the leaders who will transform decadence into enlightenment.

Dedicated Politicians

There are good reasons why many politicians are held in low esteem, but there are equally good reasons why we should be grateful to the dedicated ones who, against much undeserved criticism, are valiantly legislating principled laws to advance human progress. They are devoted, honorable public servants who work hard to improve our welfare and provide us with the gift of stable government. Although our democracy is riddled with foolish wrangling and occasional corruption, it is still the best form of government compared to all others. Perhaps it's too much to say "God bless the politicians," but neither should we be too quick to condemn them. We couldn't get along without them. They are the lifeblood of our democracy, at the forefront in the battle against cultural degeneration.

Peace Corps Volunteers

These dedicated people have embraced the wisdom of Universal Spirituality much as the early Christians embraced the essential wisdom of Christ. During the past thirty-eight years, some 165,000 men and women have planted new seeds in ninety countries. They faced harsh, sometimes primitive, conditions as they taught their expertise in agriculture, education, health, business and ecology. They showed us how to forge a brotherhood despite cultural, racial, and religious differences. We should be grateful for these pioneers for teaching us how to use the international brotherhood for bringing diverse peoples into cooperative, spiritual action.

Good Samaritans during Crises

Most human beings are "good Samaritans." This is the latent weapon that will eventually overwhelm the menacing minority. The proof of this untapped goodness is most evident during times of crisis. People from all races, faiths, and walks of life rush to help strangers —such as the victims of floods, fires, earthquakes, hurricanes, and tornadoes. Shifting to a more organized basis, it is heartwarming to see dedicated people from dozens of private and public agencies pitching in wholeheartedly to care for the injured and homeless—Universal Spirituality in action. It is a challenge for us all to let our stored-up benevolence flow more abundantly during normal daily activities. This reservoir of human kindness could bring world healing to our ailing society.

PART

2

Through the Eyes of a Spiritual Evolutionist

Chapter **10**

Spiritual Musings on the

Pathless Unknown

Where Did We Come From and
Where Are We Going?

How the universe began is beyond human conjecture, and we should leave the question alone; but how the human species originated on earth is within the realm of prudent human speculation. Based on scientific evolution, we can theorize that the human species was formed from a configuration of atoms that evolved through the mineral, plant, and animal kingdoms until it individualized into self-conscious man.

Some intuitive spiritual evolutionists picture the development of the human species as a progression of having slept in the mineral, dreamed in the plant, awakened in the animal state, and then evolved into the human form. Finally, after countless millennia, man progressed from instinct to intellect, and then assumed the dominant role over all other species on Earth.

But where are we going? The civilizing journey began with heathens appeasing and pleasing various gods with animal and human sacrifices. Eventually, these practices evolved into the One God ideal and then fragmented into worshiping Him within different religions. But human beings took a wrong turn on this journey when, instead of sharing their religious wisdoms, they dogmatized and began warring about them.

However, in spite of their divisive flaws, religions have civilized planet Earth. The people within each religion were imbued with values and virtues that fulfilled their lives. But religious leaders did not have the wisdom to reconcile their differences into a Universal Spirituality and instead whipped up hate to protect their turfs. This meant that wars and persecutions eclipsed centuries of good works within religions. And to this day, the religious leaders are using their exclusivity to divide people, as in the Middle East, India/Pakistan, and Northern Ireland.

What is needed to end the wars, based on religious intolerance, is a powerful ideal as revolutionary as the One God idea, the Ten Commandments, or Jesus' Love One Another. Such a culture-changing ideal is slowly emerging to meet the tribulations of our planet. An increasing number of people who have lost interest in traditional religions are finding a fulfilling concept of God that is more intimate and credible than the one they rejected. It combines the ancient wisdom of the prophets, the distilled inspirations of mainstream religions, and today's scientific evolutionary knowledge.

The two core characteristics of the new version of God are: 1. God is not a phantom of the universe; God is the universe, a Cosmic Energy that has intentionality, purpose, and super intelligence that guides the creative processes of the universe; 2. Evolution is the vehicle by which God as Cosmic Energy creates and re-creates new forms and expands the consciousness of all its entities. Just as the wisdom of evolution has periodically spurred mankind toward enlightened idealism, so Universal Spirituality will be the ideal to guide us to our future enlightenment.

Spiritual Evolution Is Evolving Alongside Physical Evolution

Man's physical evolution has been evolving for millions of years, but his spiritual evolution is only several thousand years old. The primary seeds of spiritual evolution were planted in the Middle East with Abraham about 5,700 years ago and in India with the Vedic tradition, approximately 1300 B. C.

Religions codified their spiritual probing in scriptural wisdom in order to give their followers something big to live for. However, with the advent of today's evolutionary science, people within and outside religions have begun to question the scriptural certainties of traditional religions.

Those on the cutting edge of spiritual evolution are appreciative of the spiritual progress religions have made but believe the time has come to evolve out of religion's divisiveness into the next stage of spiritual evolution: Universal Spirituality.

The future of spiritual evolution lies with traditional religions. They are the most numerous, and they are the most qualified to make the transformation from their limited denominational wisdom into the vaster cosmic wisdom of Universal Spirituality. Their traditional courtship with God will enable them to form the spiritual marriage with God, embracing the wisdom of all religions.

The millions who will make these spiritual transformations will effect as giant a change in spiritual evolution as Cro-Magnon man made in physical evolution by evolving into modern man.

And as we keep probing the meaning of spiritual evolution, our progress will be as unlimited as evolution itself.

The Contrast between a Cosmic–Energy God and a Fundamentalist God

I view my thinking and breathing as energy flowing through my mind and body from a cosmic source, thinned down for my human use. This flow of cosmic energy is my God—a more visible and intimate reality than viewing God through ceremonializing and singing hymns. It edges me closer to the thinking of seers who penetrate the Cosmic Energy, or God, on a much deeper level than mere, respectable, church attendance.

When I compare my way of personalizing God with the way I used to worship and the way "fundamentalists" do, I come up with these observations: Fundamentalists are as sincere as I am in embracing God, but my way is open to other views; theirs is closed. My belief has the grandeur of an evolutionary journey with eons of life-times ahead of me; theirs stops in a vague heaven. My way puts me in personal charge of my evolution; they are content to follow prescribed rules. I gratefully accept the essential wisdom of all religions; they often have an ingrained hostility toward other religions. I respect their views; I don't think they respect mine. I accept differences with the resilience of my evolutionary views; they, not believing in evolution, are more apt to react to differences with prejudice, hostility, and violence.

Cosmic Energy Is Our Source of Life

Just as a power station at the edge of town thins down its energy when it reaches an electric bulb, so cosmic energy is attenuated as it is distributed to the minimal needs of all living entities on Earth. A minuscule fragment of it comes down to man in the form of breathing and thinking. Without this spark of cosmic energy to sustain us, we would have no body, mind, or spirit—no existence. Yet we take our breathing and thinking for granted, not realizing they are our source of life. Atheists, who deny God, are not aware that their very denial is cosmic energy, God in action.

Whether we're aware of it or not, cosmic energy is constantly renewing us in proportion to our cooperation with its harmonious action. When the mind is not aware of its source of life and the body abuses its wisdom, the renewal process is inhibited, resulting in a debilitated body and barren mind. When we acknowledge, cooperate, and communicate with the Originating Source, the renewal energy flows more abundantly, resulting in a harmoniously functioning life.

Agnosticism Leads to Neither Here, There, Nor Anywhere

It is understandable that we differ over abortion, over more or less government, and over other secular and moral issues that divide us; but it's shortsighted to dismiss the role of God with the assertion "I'm an agnostic" and stop there. It's like being satisfied with shadows in a cave and not exploring what's outside.

The fact that we can't ever know the ultimate nature of God is no excuse to shrug it off with mere agnosticism. Nor should we be looking for certainty; that's as shortsighted as agnosticism. But we *should* be probing, the basic wisdom of evolutionary progress.

There's little most of us can do to affect the building

of a space station or how much to allot for foreign aid, but we can do a lot about what undergirds our own lives. Most of us are decisive about our concerns regarding family and friends, so why shouldn't we be just as decisive about our *ultimate* concern, from which all other concerns flow, probing for the meaning of spiritual evolution?

Rushing to Change Beliefs Can Lead to Escapism

Prudence is the key to successful transformation—a combination of self-mastery and daring. That's what it takes to give up past beliefs for new ones. Self-mastery means *steering* to a port—not letting the waves take us there. Daring is the willingness to give up what we have believed for something new, like the caterpillar that gives up the comfort of its cocoon to become a butterfly. But rushing to change is escapism, and many that rush to join a cult or follow a guru are not seeking genuine transformation, but are simply escaping to something different.

I've not been dazzled by quick change. My own came ploddingly, more like the slow turtle than the dashing hare. I've lifted the heavy plaster of my religious conditioning a little at a time—not in one big rip.

There are very few genuine sudden transformations. Evolution works slowly, majestically. Saul of Tarsus' sudden change to St. Paul is a rarity. Few are transformed so swiftly; most evolve slowly; and some don't change at all. But eventually, even the sluggards wake up in future incarnations. Nothing and no one thwarts evolution.

Why We Should View Impermanence with Equanimity

When we understand and accept the operating law of impermanence, life becomes less hectic and more orderly. The wisdom of this law can blunt the sting of disappointments and discomforts as well as the pain of parting with attachments. By developing a state of mind to view the parade of human events with an alert passivity, we can enjoy more equanimity and the poise to see impermanence in its true light.

To me, the wisdom of impermanence means that I don't shout my success from the rooftops, or agonize over my failures in the basement. I center my life in the living-room. I'm more aware that there is going to be rough terrain on my evolutionary path, but I also know that there will be tree-lined vistas as well.

This does not mean that I rely apathetically on fate. I work hard, as though I'm intensely ambitious—but without palpitating ambition. Or, paraphrasing St. Francis of Assisi's wisdom, I know the difference between what I can and what I can't do. Occasionally I try the impossible, but always allowing lots of room for failure.

The Soul Needs the Grist of Human Experience to Evolve

My soul—the real me, the permanent atom that survives the body, my individualized consciousness that continues its existence—needs my human experience for its ongoing evolution. It guides me with what it has learned from the past and prods me to open future frontiers.

Because I possess free will and am beset with many uncertainties, I often find it difficult to make choices, especially when my soul is confronted with a problem for which it has not acquired wisdom from the past or the present.

For example, I recently had to make a difficult choice: do I risk two million dollars to rejuvenate an old office building in a rundown neighborhood? It would provide modern office space at below-market rentals for American-trained Third World doctors and for social agencies engaged in rehabilitating drug addicts, alcoholics, the mentally ill, and pregnant teenagers—agencies that could not afford prevailing high rents. It was a hazardous financial venture, but a tempting challenge.

Arrayed against this socially desirable venture were these financial risks: the building was 50 percent vacant and losing $200,000 a year; it was smeared with graffiti and had occasionally been peppered by drive-by BB-gun shooters; and it would be difficult to raise a two-million dollar loan under these negative circumstances.

My soul's eager prodding for new experiences prompted me to put extra effort into this risky, pro-bono venture. After four turndowns, I obtained the two-million-dollar loan and went to work. I rejuvenated the neglected structure into a Class-A building and leased the vacant office space to social agencies and Third World doctors. It became an international home for the doctors and a Mecca for low-budget social agencies.

The building is now a beehive of activity—people helping people in modern, comfortable, low-budget office space. In addition to enriching my soul, the project brought a dying building back to life and upgraded a rundown neighborhood. And instead of losing $200,000 a year, the building is showing a small profit. Everyone gained, especially yours truly!

Eastern Self–Effacement Is Wiser than Western Self–Assertiveness

Having been geared to grow up with the practical philosophy of getting ahead with aggressive self-assertiveness, I considered self-effacement mystically impractical when I met it in Eastern literature. But its esoteric challenge intrigued me. The more I dug under its surface, the more I became convinced of its spiritual wisdom.

The Western penchant for rugged individualism squares with the aphorism that assertive action gets results and is the key to success. But it's in sharp contrast to Eastern wisdom, which claims that self-effacement keeps the ego in check and directs its energy through wiser channels.

I'm now convinced that low-key action is not a withdrawal from life; on the contrary, it draws us deeper into it. Quieting the ego soothes the emotions, releases more energy, and awakens the consciousness to a more caring way of life.

Self-forgetfulness does not negate the self. It makes it more effective by conserving energy rather than squandering it bombastically with showy intensity. Self-effacement develops clarity, efficiency, poise, and tranquillity. And its energy tends to flow more abundantly toward selflessness rather than selfishness.

Being a product of the West, but having absorbed some Eastern wisdom, I'm trying to strike a balance—muting my self-assertiveness but seeing that my Eastern view does not steer me into apathy. It's an adventurous straddle.

Meekness Is Not Weakness

I interpret Jesus' "Blessed are the meek, for they shall inherit the earth" to mean that those who have conquered much of their lower human nature will inherit a higher level of consciousness—spiritual wisdom.

What is the nature of this higher level of consciousness? It is an attitude toward life that makes it unnecessary to assert oneself aggressively. It is a form of self-effacing gentleness that bears no relation to subservience. On the contrary, it is a gentle strength that reins in the ego to quell its combative nature.

It is not easy to "inherit the earth." It has to be done with a strong will, because the selfish, assertive ego is a wily adversary. It can best be bridled with the wisdom of alert detachment, watching for it to rear up and then vanquishing it with the meekness of spiritual strength.

I try to use the "meekness" wisdom. It works. Some of my eye-for-an-eye competitors and associates think I'm a mat for people to step on. They're wrong. They're not familiar with the wisdom of meekness. By not countering deviousness with deviousness, greed with greed, I harvest a double-win: I advance my spirituality *and* enhance my secular success. Spiritual meekness is a powerful persuader. Jesus proved it.

The Bright and Dark Sides of Intellect

When the human species evolved from instinct to intellect, it took a giant evolutionary leap, opening vistas for creative thinking and action. This yielded a Buddha, a Jesus, an Einstein—but also a Genghis Khan, a Hitler, and a Stalin.

85

We are somewhere in between, buffeted by intellect, wavering between the sublime and the malevolent. Intellect's dark side has grown into an untamed monster, irrationally persuading millions to kill each other for the love of God, as well as manipulating us into ideological wars. The bright side of intellect, on the other hand, is inspiring men and women to care for one another in loving ways that the most exalted literature could not match.

Intellect, with its built in free-will, is a gift that can advance mankind or a curse to create human misery. The wisdom of religion has held much of intellect's irrationality at bay for centuries, but its antidotal strength is waning. Evolution's wisdom, however, is coming to the fore with a new universal spiritual ideal that will inspire and protect us from intellectual irrationalities.

The Cosmic God Is Replacing the God of Fear and Morality

Fear is a powerful motivator. It started in primitive times with fear of hunger, wild animals, and death. These fears caused primitive man to fashion a God of fear who had to be appeased to win His favor. He was worshiped with ceremonials and sacrifices.

As civilized people began to long for divine guidance to overcome their mortal fallibilities, their yearning evolved into a God who punished sin and rewarded virtue with a good life after death. This anthropomorphic God of morality succeeded the God of fear and is still deeply ingrained in today's mainstream religions.

The new version of God that is succeeding the God of morality is the Cosmic Energy God of evolution. This

God uses nondivisive Universal Spirituality to elevate individual virtue as well as guide the human race into a newly enlightened age. Spiritual scientists like Einstein, Schrödinger, and Eddington crossed the barriers of denominational religion by claiming that their awe for the cosmic spiritual experience was the strongest and noblest driving force behind their scientific research—thus pioneering the belief in the Cosmic God of the future.

The Difference between Believing in God and Surrendering to God's Will

Believing in God is primarily motivated by the prevailing cultural acceptance that it's proper and respectable to believe in the existence of God. Surrendering to God has a more dynamic motivation. It is a decision to surrender our own will and become a channel for God's will. Surrendering to God is virtuous when the wisdom of nondivisive spirituality is expressed in nondemonstrative, noncondemning ways that are cleansed of all motivations except to advance mankind, when the human will recognizes the superiority of God's will and shows it by focusing on solving secular human needs.

Surrendering to God's will is most effective when God's gentle will is given priority over intense human will. Fundamentalist Jews, Muslims, and Christians corrupt their love of God when they give priority to their human will over God's will. That's when prejudice and cruelty against different believers reveal themselves. It is only when man has unconditionally spiritualized his love of God that he can surrender unreservedly to God.

Denominational Religion Is Not Easily Abandoned

Thirty years ago, Harvey left home to find something bigger to live for than his Jewish religion. He wandered across the world, supporting himself with odd jobs along the way. He had dated my daughter when they were in high school, and because I befriended him, he called me several times during the early years of his odyssey. Then I lost track of him. At my daughter's thirty-fifth high school reunion, he showed up with his wife, and I invited them to my home.

I was shocked. The young wanderer in search of universal meaning appeared in full Chassidic regalia: round black hat, long beard, and his wife with shaven head covered with a white kerchief.

After a few preliminaries, I asked in amazement, "Harvey, what happened?"

"I found my roots," he replied.

"What roots? Where? How?"

"After wandering across America, Europe and India, where I studied with gurus and joined ashrams, I found myself sick, hungry, and exhausted on a street in Tel Aviv, Israel. A man took me into his home and fed me, and after I rested, he put twillin [a small leather cube with leather tongs that Orthodox Jews use during prayers] on my arm. There was a flash of revelation when he finished. I found what I was looking for all my life: my roots and the God of Abraham."

"But way back, Alan Ginsburg's poem 'Howl' was your God."

"That was a passing fancy, as all my other meaningless experiences had been. Judaism has always been murmuring in my blood, but I had been listening only with my head. Now I've surrendered to Judaism with my heart."

"To an anthropomorphic God?" I asked.

"Yes, to an anthropomorphic God."

I turned to his wife. "What about you? How did you come to this conviction?"

"The same way. Like Harvey, I too roamed about India, but I couldn't find God there. When I met Harvey in Brooklyn fifteen years ago, I found God and a husband, in that order. We now live in Crown Point, both of us teaching children to live authentic Chassidic lives."

The three major markings on the evolutionary journey are instinct, which guides animals; reason, which guides man; and religion, which has guided us beyond reason. It has taken millennia to evolve instinct, about fifteen thousand years to initiate reason, and about six thousand years to plant the seeds of religion. And it will take many centuries to integrate Universal Spirituality before it is accepted as the fourth marking to guide us into the future.

The Difference between Personality and Individuality

The personality is the visible demeanor on the outside. The individuality is the less visible characteristic on the inside. Together they comprise the total person. The individuality is a summation of the distilled talents and values of previous incarnations, while the personality grows out of the indigenous physical and cultural environment.

I have encountered businessmen and professionals with the most blah personalities but whose sterling qualities showed no sign on the outside. And I know people with the most winning personalities who are hollow on the inside. And on many occasions I've seen people with pleasing personalities that matched their virtuous individualities—an extraordinary combination.

I recall that when I was a student, the ones who always raised their hands to show the little they knew impressed me less than the students who knew more but showed it only when called upon. I began formulating the difference between personality and individuality way back then.

Gandhi and Einstein inherited the values and talents of their individualities from former lifetimes but not their personalities. Hitler mesmerized millions with his personality, while his underdeveloped individuality was still struggling to evolve from bestiality.

Individuality is close to the soul's wisdom and is at the edge of Universal Spirituality. Recognizing the difference between individuality and personality is a valuable asset in forming social and business relationships.

The Survival of the Fittest

The survival of the physically fittest is gone; the supremacy of the technologically elite is here. What's next?

Fifteen thousand years ago, man followed herds of reindeer to eat and fought off wild beasts to keep from being eaten. The physically fittest survived. Today, a hundred-pound woman terrorist with a machine gun can kill a dozen of the most physically fit men. And several berserk terrorists could destroy a city's population with one nuclear bomb.

We are living in the age of technology. The masters of high tech are in charge of the world's transportation, information, and communication. They also provide the latest mechanical marvels for our creature comforts. And they are about to wire us into one global village.

But the wisdom of evolution is ringing bells of alarm. The dark side of technology is ravaging the Earth and menacing the lives of millions with its deadly weapons of mass destruction. Technology and unbridled science have the power to send us back to the age of the survival of the fittest.

Fortunately, scientists who believe in the survival of the *wisest* are awakening the world to use its technology to save us from potential destruction. Good and evil technologies are locked in a desperate struggle, and the good can win only if the spiritually wise will prevail. At stake is whether technological progress will usher in a new age to meet the needs of more people or a dark age of global conflagration.

Evolution Provides for All Endings to Have New Beginnings

There isn't a beginning that doesn't have an ending, except the beginningless and endingless universe. Coping with endings of conditions to which we're attached—a good job, an enjoyable relationship, a comfortable home, or the life of a loved one—is a painful experience that can best be healed with an optimistic belief in new beginnings.

It's easy to discuss or write about the liberating effect of non-attachment, of accepting change, but human attachment is not some fluffy stuff easily blown away; it's cement on the mind. However, there is a way to crack and chip it away, a healing power that's more effective than psychiatric reasoning. It's a cosmic wisdom which convinces us that overcoming losses is the grist and inevitability of evolutionary progress.

If we face the sorrowing over what might have been with the conviction that there's a lesson to be learned in an ending, then the healing comes from a recognition that this is the way evolutionary wisdom is forged. This is much more than secular logic. It's the wise acceptance of endings and the belief in new beginnings. It's the basis for the realistic optimism that death is the gateway to a new beginning.

Federate the Israelis, Palestinians, and Jordanians into a Greater Palestine

During one of my meditations, I stumbled on an idea that may seem naive but that could be a practical way to avoid a war between the Israelis and Arabs.

Seven hundred years ago, the Germans, French, and Italians fought bloody battles for pieces of what is now Switzerland. Eventually, enlightened leaders from each group federated the disputed land into what it is today. The French settled around Lausanne, the Germans around Zurich, and the Italians around Lugano.

What a persuasive example for the Israelis, Palestinians, and Jordanians to "Switzerlandize" into a federation of what was formerly known as Greater Palestine!

Naive? Ridiculous? Yes, for the present hostile generation of Arabs and Israelis who are blindly clinging to territorial holiness and zealous religious beliefs. But it will not be naive or ridiculous for the future generations of leaders on both sides who will see with enlightened wisdom that those who respect and meet each other's needs will live in peace, while those who cling fanatically to holy pasts condemn themselves to war and human misery.

The new leaders will get to the core of the conflict by recognizing the profound fact that they came from the same Originating Source and are yearning for the same God—Allah or Jehovah. They will educate the masses to realize that by freeing themselves of ancient hatreds, Greater Palestine could become the democratic industrial jewel of the Middle East. All would gain. Cooperation would replace the chaos that is now heading into a collision with catastrophe. It's not too early to begin laying the foundation for a Greater Palestine.

Chapter 11

A Medley of Insights

Initiated During Meditation

Awareness Is an Ordinary Word Brimming with Extraordinary Wisdom

About forty years ago, when I was panting with ambition, I made a pitch to a bank president to appoint me as his broker to sell the bank's foreclosed properties. I did most of the talking, he most of the listening. He was aware of what was going on in his mind and mine. I debated, he observed.

I didn't get the assignment.

The contrast between his poised awareness and my palpitations left an indelible mark on my mind.

It was ten years later and I was somewhat wiser. An irate three-month rent-delinquent tenant stormed into my office and berated me as a "sleazy" landlord. I listened calmly to his tirade without condemning his false accusations. I used what I had learned from the banker. The tenant slammed the door and left. Several years later he came to my office, a different man.

"I want to apologize for the way I ranted against you. You responded with such quiet sensitivity . . . I never forgot it. Here is my delinquent rent," he said, putting a check on my desk.

"What happened?" I asked in amazement.

"I found God." A long discussion followed, and we became fast friends.

Awareness is different from consciousness. Consciousness is passive; awareness is active. To be conscious is to see the presence of a person in isolation from his or her surroundings. To be aware is to absorb the subtle nuances, the wider background surrounding the consciousness. Awareness observes without opinionating. The ego is muted, not activated into a confrontation. To be aware of the importance of awareness opens doors to spiritual understanding.

Trusting People Is a Gamble Worth Taking

I've come to realize that the more suspicious I was of people, the more suspicious they were of me. And the more I dwelt on protecting myself from ulterior motives, the more I found them in others. After one of my meditative sessions, I made a major decision: I would trust more, live more vulnerably, and relax rather than mistrust and live invulnerably with tension. I've tested my theory many times; it works.

I allowed a young woman to sign checks in one of my apartment complexes after I learned that she had a somewhat checkered past, but with the inducement that if she performed honestly, I would help her turn the corner in an accounting career. She accepted my trust gratefully, but two years later I learned that she had swindled someone out of $8,000 while she was working for me. I had my accountant look into her two years of check-signing and found no loss. When she left, I concluded that her honesty was my repayment for trusting her.

Has it always worked? No. I've been conned by a photographer for $10,000, by an antique dealer for $5,000, by a computer guru for $8,000. But against the few who didn't reciprocate my trust, there have been hundreds of others who responded in ways that resulted in quality relationships and mutually profitable deals.

My experience convinced me that the more we harbor suspicion, the more we'll perpetuate it in others. The more we open ourselves to others, the more they'll open themselves to us.

If You're Looking for Identity, Don't Look for Ancestral Roots

I can't go back further than my grandfather, yet I don't feel any loss of identity. I don't understand all this fuss about the importance of identity. To me, the important question is not "Who am I?" but "What am I doing with my life?"

Those who strut their memberships in exclusive clubs, content to ride on their ancestors' coattails instead of spreading their own wings, as well as those who live off the bounty of birthrights and titles, deserve only our passing nods, not scraping bows.

High or low ancestral beginnings do not an identity make. No need digging into our past roots. Our identities are already established, stamped indelibly by the experiences of previous lifetimes and beckoning us to more radiant existences in lifetimes to come. The open-ended reincarnational view gives us a believable account of where we are, who we are, and where we're going.

Forgetting Our Psychological Past Alleviates Human Misery

There are two kinds of memory: the functional and the psychological. The functional is the mundane remembering of how to fix a furnace, fly an airplane, cook a meal, keep an appointment, and the like. The psychological is an accumulation of memories about people and past events. These memories are prone to fester, swell, rupture, and spread into confrontation, hate, and violence.

I had a discussion on this subject with a successful young businessman. "I never forget an insult, a put-down, or when someone throws a curve at me. I slip it into my memory, and when the time is right, I pay it back in spades," he boasted.

"But wouldn't emptying revengeful thoughts from your mind lower your blood pressure?"

"Maybe . . . but if a guy spits in my eye, am I to wipe it off and forget it? We're built to fight back, and thank God my memories help me do it."

"Have you ever stopped to think how our psychological memories create misery in the world?"

"Psychological memories . . . what's that?"

"Not the memories we need for our daily chores, but memories that harden into political, religious, and racial prejudices—hostile memories that divide people."

"You're carrying this psychological memory business too far; you're too visionary."

"Is it too visionary to get rid of hostile garbage thoughts instead of carrying the slop in your memory?"

"But that's like asking me to fly. I can't fly."

"There was a time when birds couldn't fly. They were earthbound vertebrates. But they learned, didn't they?"

"But it took eons of years!"

"But they DID it! We've got to start sometime. If we're to save ourselves from ourselves, we'll have to learn how to get rid of our psychological pasts. They're loaded with dangerous baggage. They've been responsible for wars and terrible atrocities."

"Oh, George, you're too idealistic, too impractical!"

"*You're* the one who's impractical. Millions like you are having their little wars all over the world. Eventually they spread and blow up into big ones."

"George, you're on a different planet— a dreamer."

Spiritual Healing Has Greater Power than Psychiatry

My understanding of Jungian literature has led me to believe that spirituality has more healing power than psychiatry. Its active ingredient of inspiration has greater capacity to reverse mental and emotional disorders than intellectual medicine does.

Psychiatrists help people adjust and endure, for which we should be grateful. But because they deal only with the intellect, their cures are limited. They do not penetrate to the deeper healing dimension. It is not easily tapped, but when you surrender your disordered mind to what you believe has the ultimate healing power—God (Cosmic Healing Power)—a transformation takes place that is often referred to as a miracle, a synonym for an unusual, accelerated cure.

Intellect carries us to the foothills of understanding, but it takes spiritual internalization to reach the mountain peak of inspirational healing. Those who rely on psychiatry learn to adjust but don't experience peace of soul—a transcendental dimension of contentment.

Relating past to present gives patients a better insight into their problems, but not the spiritual energy of changing disequilibrium into equilibrium. The Jungian spiritual healing process advances psychiatry from a two-dimensional to a three-dimensional power. We see more, feel more, understand more.

Anyone Can Become a Healer

Physicians and psychiatrists need not have a monopoly on healing. If we rely solely on them, we'll have a permanent epidemic of sickness. Medical science has improved our health, and we should be grateful for it, but unless we learn a few basic insights on how to heal others and ourselves, we'll continue to fill hospitals and rely on doctors and pills to treat our ills.

How can we become healers? By paying attention to a few natural laws on how diseases form and how to get rid of them. For example, do we really need doctors to tell us that alcohol, tobacco, and drugs defile our bodies; that conniving, revenge, and hate warp our minds? Yet like lemmings that rush into the sea to die, we thoughtlessly drive ourselves into early death by not avoiding these health-sapping traps.

We practice preventive medicine when we heal others by praising, giving, and forgiving. We heal ourselves when we learn to accept resistance with detachment rather than fighting it with fear. We can accelerate healing by becoming aware that the most miraculous surgery within our bodies is performed without the aid of doctors. We heal ourselves when we become convinced that such mundane matters as a carnivorous diet and lack of exercise cause ill health.

Jesus' prescription to love one another was good medicine for his time, and it's still the most powerful healing advice for our time.

The "I Want It Now" Syndrome Is Debilitating Our Society

Instant action, without thought for the future, was all right for the savage, but not for modern man. Giving up tomorrow for "now" is not a good deal.

A real estate developer I dealt with caught an inflationary wave and rode it to a multi-million-dollar fortune. Ignoring the future, he bought a $500,000 home, a private plane, and a condo in the Bahamas. A few years later, during an economic downturn, he lost it all in bankruptcy. He was dazzled by the immediate and fizzled away his future.

One of my real-estate salesmen was too impatient to wait for real romance with *one,* and chose instant gratification with *many.* He paid the price years later for his excessive "nows" with a lonely single life, envying my other salesmen, who were enjoying their families. And millions of drug, alcohol, and gambling addicts are paying the price for their "I want it now!" with broken bodies and broken lives.

To do away with instant gratification is as wise as waiting for cars to pass before crossing a street.

A Quiet Mind Has More Clarity than a "Monkey" or "Cow" Mind

There was a time when my chattering "monkey mind" thoughts controlled me. Trying to stop them was as futile as trying to hold back the wind. Often they were so overwhelming that, as hard as I tried to think them away, they—not I—became the masters of my mind. They drove my voluntary will into involuntary bedlam. They drained my energies and obscured my business judgment.

While looking for a way to quiet my monkey mind, I became aware of the opposite danger—the "cow" mind. I didn't want that either. People with cow-like apathy barely raise an eyebrow at anything exciting. They're satisfied to chew a few thoughts with as little concern as cows pasturing in the meadow. Their life is mostly like a morning fog—few rainbows.

Peace at the price of a cow mind was not for me. I wanted a quiet mind cleansed of monkey chatter but without cow-like indifference. I found it in meditation—quieting my mind's activity for a half-hour a day in a quiet corner of my home. It's not easy to stop distracting thoughts in their tracks. All kinds of mundane opinions clamor for attention; but with perseverance I tamed the tumult.

With years of meditation, I have been able to flush out most of my monkey mind thoughts and replace them with the valuable insights that launched me on my open-ended quest to understand the wisdom of spiritual evolution.

We Need an Economic System that Decentralizes Megalopolises

You who live on a farm, in a village or small town—count your blessings! You're closer to a natural living environment than people living in congested megalopolises. The human species took a wrong turn on its evolutionary journey when it lurched into emulating a queen-bee society, where the drones work feverishly for the queen and her attendants.

Man has created materialistic marvels, but he's neglected to structure an economy where people can work and live in a spacious environment. Living in congested concrete jungles deprives people of the enjoyment of trees, flowers, and grass. Their racing thoughts have little opportunity for reflection, for meaning, for creating deep friendships. Scientists have shown that when rodents live in close quarters, they become cannibalistic, and when given more room, they live peacefully. These scientists draw the conclusion that there is a similarity between the behaviors of mice and men.

In contrast to how urban man dehumanizes his environment is this view from a chief of a North American Indian tribe: "Every part of this Earth is sacred to my people . . . every shining pine needle . . . every sandy shore . . . every mist in the dark woods . . . every meadow . . . every humming insect—all are holy to my people."

T. S. Eliot sums up our predicament when he asks in this poem "The Rock":

Where is the life we lost in living?
Where is the wisdom we have lost in knowledge?
Where is the knowledge we lost in information?
The cycles of heaven in twenty centuries
Bring us farther from God and nearer to dust.

It's More Important to Change Human Nature than Institutions

We've overemphasized the importance of changing institutions and underestimated the significance of changing people. One deals with surface, the other with depth. Bad people can corrupt the best institution. You can't make a good omelet with bad eggs.

Though laws and political systems modify human nature to some extent, they do not effect a profound change. Did the Russian people change after the bloody revolution by which they cleansed themselves of czarism and converted to communism? Weren't Stalin and his hordes crueler than the czar?

When Republicans take over from Democrats, or vice versa, do the leaders and their followers change? Do the advocates of the far right, with their conservative views, or the champions of the far left, with their liberal views, have any programs for elevating human nature?

Changing human nature is the forgotten factor of our civilization. We forget, at our peril, that two thousand years ago a wise man gave his life to show that it is more crucial to spiritualize humanity than to cling to self-righteous religious institutions. His wisdom profoundly changed more lives than all the changes made by all the institutions during the past twenty centuries.

Why Didn't Religion Evolve as Fast as Science?

I discussed this subject with an avowed fundamentalist who was also a scientist—a Jewish doctor of internal medicine.

G. B. Why would a modern scientist like you want to cling to primitive orthodox religious rules?

Dr. I have a simple answer. I want to renew Judaism in its pristine form, in its original One God wisdom that has civilized my people. There's your answer, direct and to the point.

G. B. It's neither direct nor to the point. Why use

the latest in medicine and stick to the oldest in religion?

Dr. Because science is different from religion. Science deals with matter; religion with the spirit. The yearning for God 5,700 years ago was the same as it is today. Why sully it with modern garbage? Don't you think an original is better than a copy?

G. B. Were the original medicine men better than modern doctors were?

Dr. You're not getting the point. The original medicine men were primitive scientists. We've improved on them. But has modern man improved on the wisdom of the Prophets? On Moses? On the Psalms? I don't find any awe or mystery in the new-fangled changes in Reform Judaism or in your Universal Spirituality. I love tradition . . . antiquity . . . the ancestral yearnings for God. Divine Jewish spirit hasn't changed. It has no expiration date. I love to feel the ancient murmuring in my blood. Are you beginning to get the difference, George?

G. B. I do. But what bothers me is that passionate fundamentalists, like you as well as people in other religions, are planting mines the world over, as has happened in Iran and is brewing in Algeria, the Middle East, and elsewhere, leading to blowups.

Dr. Are you suggesting assimilation, God forbid?

G. B. I'm not suggesting assimilation. But wouldn't we have a more peaceful world if fundamentalist leaders of ALL religions merged their religious differences in a Universal Spirituality? Their hostility toward each other is irreligious, sinful. Passionate orthodoxy kills; Universal Spirituality heals. Why not investigate the most progressive step in religious evolution?

Dr. And second-fiddle our history, our Covenant

with God? Never! My religious security is real, built on time-tested wisdom. Yours is ephemeral, built on sand.

G. B.   No. Yours is built on the past; mine on the future.

Uncertainty—the Key Wisdom of Evolution

Uncertainty and creativity are intertwined. One cannot exist without the other. It's at the heart of evolutionary wisdom. It propels us toward understanding our relationship with God, man, and the universe.

Creativity would cease if by some magic wand we could know in advance the detailed outcome of a business venture, a love affair, what type of work we'd be doing, how our children would turn out, and dozens of other uncertainties that keep confronting us.

Most people prefer the comfort of certainty—a secure job, an institutionalized religion, a stable life. There's nothing wrong with wanting these certainties; but we dare not put them in deep freeze. We should be ready to live vulnerably, to welcome uncertainties as friends, not enemies, because they help us chart new directions for new experiences to enrich our lives.

For instance, I didn't know, after spending hundreds of hours writing this book, whether it would be good enough to be published. But even if I failed, the many hours I spent on it enabled me to dredge up valuable insights that never would have crossed my mind had I not risked the unknown. Uncertainties are filled with opportunities, whether they fall on the credit or debit side of the ledger.

The Difference between Preference
and Prejudice

Only spiritually evolved sages have no preferences—they love all humanity. Yet even they are apt to prefer conversing with spiritual people to conversing with ignorant ones. Our parents and peers with their preferences condition most of us. As a result, these preferences become so deeply ingrained in us that it would be foolhardy to expect Jews not to prefer to live among Jews, Muslims among Muslims, wealthy among wealthy, poor among poor, and Afro-Americans among their own. There's nothing prejudicial about preferring relationships with one's kin.

What turns preferences into prejudices is not having evolved enough to appreciate and enjoy diversity—different mannerisms, looks, values, cultures, and religions. Differences are the natural outgrowth of evolution, the teaching materials for human progress.

Prejudice is a devolution in human character. Its suffocating vision of life condemns its practitioners to self-isolation when they turn away from others outside their myopic view. It takes a spiritual shift to change from prejudice to preference, as it does to change from preference to enjoying relationships on a wider and more diverse scale.

In the mean time, let us understand the reasons for prejudices, enjoy our preferences, and savor the emerging freedom to experience the varied cultural treasures of diversity in our midst.

The Profound Wisdom of Common Sense

Common sense has the intuitive understanding of what is right and wrong about our personal, social, economic, and moral problems. It's at the edge of spiritual wisdom.

I've seen firsthand how common sense operated in others and in myself. Thirty-five years ago, my brother-in-law hit upon the common-sense idea of insuring the upper 20 percent of home mortgages. It had never been done before. He figured it would provide more security for lenders and lower the down-payment for buyers. After several years of overcoming many difficulties, he went public with it. Fifteen years ago, he sold the Mortgage Guaranty Co. for 1.2 billion dollars. His common-sense idea increased home ownership for thousands of families.

Fifty years ago, a friend of mine got the idea of providing temporary help to companies that periodically needed it. This common-sense concept took off immediately, and he expanded nationally, then internationally. It is the present Milwaukee-based Manpower, Inc. It employs close to a million part-time workers—more than any of the Fortune 500 companies.

On a much smaller scale, I've tried to use common sense in my real-estate business. I became aware that old buildings, like old generals, fade away into disuse because most owners don't have the imagination to recycle them into new uses at a profit. During the past fifty years, I've bought several dozen hundred-year-old buildings (at 10 percent of what it would have cost to replace them), rehabbed their Old-World charm, rented space at one-third the price of new structures, and realized returns from 20 to 50 percent on my investments. This common-sense idea breathed new life into old buildings, upgraded neighborhoods, supplied low-rental office space for first-time entrepreneurs, and provided millions of dollars of work for craftsmen.

Some forty years ago, when I built and fully leased the first modern office building in Milwaukee, I received requests to build office buildings in other cities. After several sessions of quiet-time meditation, I decided to forgo the offers, earn less money, and spend more time with my wife and three children. It was the best common-sense decision I made in my life.

Will Global Communication Divide or Unite Mankind?

Will millions in remote villages of underdeveloped countries who have been shut off from world events and ideas be maneuvered by global communication to stir up hostility against people they'll never see in the flesh? Or will they be encouraged to develop empathy for people of different races, cultures, and religions? Like most technologies, instant communication—a relatively new phenomenon—can be used benevolently to elevate society or malevolently to drag it down into greater divisiveness.

Planetary communication has conditioned us to form hostile views of people from Iran, Syria, Iraq, and Libya. And it has whipped up hostility among the Muslims toward the West. The media are more interested in focusing on the sensational than on the virtuous, because there's more profit in covering the shocking news than in covering the good news. Ratings are higher for the sordid details about Rodney King, O. J. Simpson, or Monica Lewinsky.

A case in point: an ecumenical event in Chicago a few years ago featured a world meeting of the Parliament of Religions that was attended by some of the wisest people on earth. The media barely gave it a nod, even though the participants offered the most practical ways to heal the festering wounds of our global society.

Instant communication is leading us toward a crucial crossroad. Spiritual men at the controls of the global media conceivably could usher in a renaissance of enlightenment; or money-hungry CEOs could push us further into the morass of antagonism and divisiveness. The stakes are high indeed. They will determine the quality of our civilization in the coming centuries.

Climbing Is More Exhilarating than Arriving

I've enjoyed climbing metaphoric mountains in dozens of successful-real estate ventures, and after each one there was a letdown. I was fired up while climbing, cooled down upon arriving. Why? Because climbing is the exciting joy of creating, while arriving is a stepped-down feeling of satisfaction.

With my real-estate projects, my imaginative juices were in flood stage when I set out to choose the right location, find low-interest financing, decide on the building's uses, develop a market plan, and, finally, mesh all these variables into a finished product that met the needs of the tenants and showed a profit. In many ways, it was more creative than writing; I touched the lives of people more directly.

Whether it's writing a book, building a bridge, or composing an opera: when it's finished, the high-energy flow of creation drops to a lower level. While recognition of results is pleasing, it does not have the inspirational high that's akin to emulating cosmic creation. Since the principal purpose of God is creation, then man is closest to God when he is creating.

From my experience, I have more than a hunch that designing a chair is more fulfilling than sitting on it; composing music more inspiring than listening to it; and sculpting jewelry more fun than wearing it. Measured on a scale of what provides fulfillment, it is safe to assume that those who find joy in creating are more in tune with Cosmic Creation than those possessing the objects of creation.

Years ago I began looking for a challenge that involved climbing without arriving— something that would keep me going without stopping. I found it in Universal Spirituality. Its challenge proved so vast that the more I probed, the more wondrous it became.

Creation Is More Exhilarating than Possession

If we believe that creation is the main purpose of God, then it follows that to be in harmony with God, the main purpose of man should also be creation within the scope of human capabilities.

Aristotle called attention to this stupendous fact when he proclaimed that man was made for creative work. On the other hand, I've not heard or read about any sage extolling possession.

I have experienced the difference between creation and possession. I converted an outdated, oil-slicked auto shop into a mini-mall of small stores; a hundred-year-old building into a business incubator for first-time entrepreneurs; and an abandoned 150,000-sq.-ft. furniture warehouse into 110 loft apartments. In all these ventures of recycling old buildings to new uses, my joy meter, on a scale of one to ten, was an enthusiastic ten.

I now own these buildings. They provide hundreds of thousands of cash-flow dollars. I have a good feeling about managing my success; but my possession-joy-meter registers only a five. Possession is passive; creation is active. It's the difference between being a spectator or a participant, a locomotive or a caboose.

I've seen proud contentment in the eyes of millionaires who possess great art, luxurious homes, expensive cars; but I've also noticed only sophisticated complacency. In contrast, I've observed the shine in a carpenter's face as he meticulously fits a wooden plank into place, the joy of a fisherman affixing his bait, and the excitement of a first-grader reciting the Pledge of Allegiance before his class for the first time.

Just as climbing is more exhilarating than arriving, so too creation, because it's in tune with the main purpose of the Cosmic Process, produces more powerful evolutionary mileage than does possession.

Business Is Not a Game, and Winning Is Not Its Name

Whoever said winning is everything may have been clever, but not wise. The winning-syndrome that has infested business has created more havoc than good.

Business has become a battle of wits in order to stave off the bombardment of government directives, union demands, consumer complaints, and competitive pressures. And when businessmen finish the year, they resent Uncle Sam's sidling up for a piece of the action. Harried and hurried, they're too busy to explore the wisdom of viewing business as an enlightened enterprise—the privilege of making a contribution to society.

I've dealt with businessmen who covered the entire spectrum of the winning-aberration from corner-cutting to lying, cheating, bribery, and embezzlement. I've seen businessmen drive themselves to the brink of coronaries and bankruptcies. Some of the super-rich are so obsessed with winning that one of their great pleasures is to leave their competitors gasping in their wake.

But business need not be a grasping struggle for conquest. An inspiring talk I heard about thirty-five years ago at a Building Owners and Managers Association conference gave me an insight into the effectiveness of mixing spiritual wisdom with business.

"I'm in the builders' supply business," the speaker said. "I have about three hundred customers, and I view them as my parishioners—my flock. Just as my pastor ministers to my spiritual needs, I minister to their commercial needs—special orders, meeting deadlines, fair pricing. They are all my friends. I don't push; I'm there only to serve. I'm successful, and—what's more important—I have a lot of fun."

The cynical businessman may raise a sophisticated eyebrow and ask: Can you deposit fun in the bank? The answer: How much is a life worth if it's polished on the outside and hollow on the inside?

Life Is a Three-Act Play

Playing the stellar role in our own life, with a cast of hundreds of supporting actors, is far more intriguing than any play staged by the most gifted playwright. That's because our storyline is "for real," and the other is make-believe.

To live our story interestingly and dramatically is the challenge we all face. To meet the challenge, we should play our scenes with verve and purpose to match the action of the greatest play ever written.

Act I   The First 30 Years: After playing the role of the curious child, the green years of a teenager, and a romantic young adult, the story enters the dramatic phase of choosing a mate and carving a career—a slice of life filled with anticipation and uncertainties.

Act II   From 30 to 60 Years: The plot thickens. Titillating temptations arise to test value choices—confrontations in relationships and work; the adoption of religious values; and many more important issues. The storyline moves forward at a slower pace as it approaches the golden years of Act. III.

Act III   60 Years and Beyond: Action begins to taper off. More contemplation, more looking backward than forward. Health begins to deteriorate but is accompanied by mocking humor: "My back goes out more than I do"; or "The elderly, white-haired lady I help across the street is my wife." Thoughts about life after death begin to creep in, along with conflicts about what to believe and what not to believe. For some who believe in reincarnation, the Golden Years are a stairway to serenity; for others, the anguish of approaching death is a saddening experience.

It's true—"All the world's a stage," and each of us plays the lead role in a real-life drama—different from any story ever written.

How Shall We View the Future in the Third Act of Our Life?

The seed that bloomed at twenty-one need not wilt at eighty. Cosmic Energy—God—still runs the show, even at that advanced age. When our life drama is in the third act, it behooves us to plan a happy ending.

I have an octogenarian friend who is a millionaire and an atheist. He shuffles along in feeble geometric steps and describes his future thus: "Where are the Golden Years? I've worked myself to a frazzle and made millions, but what good are they? I can't digest the food I like, I'm too feeble to travel, half my organs hurt, and the rest don't work. There's nothing more to life than a bitter end and oblivion." My friend has talked himself into a despair of his own making.

We have the choice of handling our future either pessimistically or optimistically. My "realistic" friend chose gloom and doom and is living his remaining years in self-inflicted hopelessness.

As an octogenarian myself, I look upon the uncertainty of my continuity with the optimistic insight that if I were to wish for the optimum condition for my life's continuation, it would fall short of what the Cosmic Wisdom—God—has in store for me. In the mean time, I enjoy the serene sense that I'm linked to the grandeur of reincarnation, with the challenge of grinding and refining the grist of my experiences into spiritual wisdom for use in this and the next incarnation.

I can't prove these open-ended grand expectations for my future, but neither can my despairing friend prove his oblivion. My spiritual intuition convinces me that my optimism is more in tune with the wisdom of progressive evolution than is my friend's pessimism. Uncertainties are filled with evolutionary possibilities.

Viewing the Ordinary with a Sense of the Sacred

When we're in a restaurant and our companion's eyes are wandering, that's a tell-tale sign that distracting thoughts are in charge of the companionship.

Lack of concentration between the observer and the observed diminishes our ability to enjoy the intimate now, where real-life action takes place free from interfering thoughts that block out the immediate. Total attention between people fuses interests and enriches relationships.

While taking a walk in my neighborhood, I noticed a carpenter installing a front door in a house. I stopped and asked: "You're so intent on what you're doing. Why?"

He put down his tools and with a relaxed smile said: "I'm glad you asked. I have a philosophy about work. I'm happiest when I measure, cut, fit, and see the result. For me, work is sacred. Am I an oddball?"

"No, you're very wise."

I've had similar encounters with men and women who fixed cars, cleaned houses, and prepared meals. The capacity to become completely absorbed in ordinary work is an extraordinary gift. To enjoy an amateur play with the same enthusiasm as viewing the best of Broadway, to listen avidly to first-graders singing off-key tunes—these are sacred moments. They encourage the amateur performers and reward the appreciative spectators—a double win.

Some of my friends beam with childlike enthusiasm at an unusual postage stamp, a rare book, a picturesque snuffbox, and a 200-year-old commode. No matter how mundane, as long as it quickens the interest, the ordinary becomes extraordinary. Or, as Thomas Moore in his book *Care of the Soul* puts it: "Viewing the ordinary with a sense of the sacred enriches the soul."

The Five Cosmic Principles That Define My Life

In my search for an overall perspective to define my life, I culled these five cosmic principles from reading, discussions, and my own reflections.

1. My human experiences are not an illusion, as some mystics claim. They are opportunities, challenges, and obstacles on the path leading to evolutionary progress.

2. My soul is the real me. It's using my body, as it has used myriad of my bodies before, to transmute my human experience into spiritual wisdom. My present incarnation has inherited the values and capacities that my soul has garnered from the past. What I experience now will be added in the next incarnation.

3. Evolution is the vehicle for my soul's progress. It started as a combination of atoms and evolved through the mineral, plant, and animal stages until it individualized and evolved into the person I am today.

4. Reincarnation is cyclical wisdom operating in the universe. That's why evolution and reincarnation are cosmically intertwined and thus assure my soul's immortality a pilgrimage that never ends.

5. God—the constant, creative Cosmic Energy—is the Universal One Life in which all else has its existence. I am part of it; and it is not whole without me.

I Was Wonderfully Led

As I stated earlier, my mother and I escaped from Russia when I was twelve years old. The experience of learning a new language and finding a niche in a strange land was as agonizing emotionally as was dodging death physically.

My life took a new turn when I found Moral Rearmament in the early 1950s. MRA's primary purpose was to seek God's guidance, during daily quiet times, for ways to elevate human nature. Its basic philosophy was to unify all religions, cultures, and races into a brotherhood of man. This aroused my interest and became the first step in developing a master plan for my life.

Hundreds of quiet-time hours led me to make several significant changes: I transmuted my belief in God from Jewish orthodoxy to Universal Spirituality; I infused my business activities with a sense of contribution rather than "the bottom line"; I made up my mind that my main purpose in life was to refine my human experience into spiritual wisdom.

The question that kept churning in my mind was: Where did the insights come from that led me to make these revolutionary changes? Over time, my secular logic, together with periods of quiet time, gave me the answer.

Here is the essence of the answer: Cosmic Energy is God, constantly renewing, healing, and guiding me, whether I'm aware of it or not. During meditation, I communicate with my Cosmic Energy God that has intentionality, purpose, and cosmic intelligence. While I am evolving on a human scale, God is advancing evolution on a cosmic scale. These reflections give me as intimate a feeling of God as any devout fundamentalist experiences, but without zealotry.

And so, because of the many wonderful things that have happened to me, I can say: "Yes, I was wonderfully led!"